JUSTICE ACCORDING TO LAW

JUSTICE ACCORDING TO LAW

by Roscoe Pound

KENNIKAT PRESS
Port Washington, N. Y./London

JUSTICE ACCORDING TO LAW

Copyright, 1951, by Yale University Press
Reissued in 1973 by Kennikat Press by arrangement
Library of Congress Catalog Card No.: 72-85285
ISBN 0-8046-1706-6

Manufactured by Taylor Publishing Company   Dallas, Texas

CONTENTS

PART I. What Is Justice? 1

PART II. What Is Law? 32

PART III. Judicial Justice 62

INDEX 93

FOREWORD

These lectures are printed as they were delivered at Westminster College. If I were to write a treatise on the administration of justice it would need many further chapters, each much longer and more full of detail than would comport with the limits of a lecture to a college audience. There would also have to be an elaborate apparatus of notes. But the detail and the notes would add little to and might very likely subtract from the impression of the purpose, method, and problems of the administration of justice according to law which I have sought to impart. That impression, derived from sixty years of practice and teaching of law, I would give *quantum valeat*, unburdened with the accumulated detailed information on the basis of which it has been formed.

R. P.

April 25, 1951
School of Law
University of California at Los Angeles

PART 1

What Is Justice?

"'What is truth?' said jesting Pilate, and would not stay for an answer." So Bacon begins his Essay on Truth. Pilate was no doubt wise according to his lights in not waiting for an answer since the two reigning philosophies of the time, the Epicurean and the doctrine of the New Academy held that there was no certain answer. Indeed, we are still debating the question. At the International Congress of Comparative Law in August of this year Pragmatists, Neo-Idealists, and the Thomists were arguing it vigorously with no sign of agreement. What is justice is another such question. Philosophers have been debating it since the Greek philosophers of the fifth century B.C. began to inquire into the nature of social control and seek a principle behind it. Daniel Webster tells us that justice is the chiefest interest of man on earth. But what justice is remains a matter of dispute in philosophy, ethics, and jurisprudence. It is significant that each of the four words most used in the science of law, namely, Justice, Rights, Law, and Morals, words for ideas at the very foundation of that science, are words upon whose meaning jurists have not been and now are unable to agree. Here also there are those who say that no answer is possible.

One, but only one, source of difficulty in each case is a poverty of terms which compels one word to carry many meanings. Right as a noun has five meanings. Law is used in at least five, and the term in the language of Continental Europe which we translate as "law" has the many meanings of Right added. Morals has two. Justice is another word of this sort.

In different theories which have been urged justice has been regarded as an individual virtue, or as a moral idea, or as a regime of social control, or as the end or purpose of social control and so of law, or as the ideal relation among men which we seek to promote and maintain in civilized society and toward which we direct social control and law as the most specialized form of social control. Definitions of justice depend upon which of these approaches is taken. Let us look at each of them.

WHAT IS JUSTICE?

Greek philosophers start with justice as an individual virtue. This idea of justice is preserved for us in the famous definition in the Institutes of Justinian: Justice is the constant and continual purpose which gives to everyone his own. Thus it is a principle of rectitude and just dealing of men with each other. Conformity of conduct to that principle, integrity, is one of the cardinal virtues. From this we got analogical uses such as the rightfulness or uprightness of something, e.g., the justice of a cause or of a position, or, again, conformity to truth or right reason or fairness, e.g., the justice of a description or of a narrative or of a judgment. By further development we get the idea of the maintenance or administration of that which is just, and hence the regime of rendering to everyone his due or his rights, or, as I prefer to say, his reasonable expectations. From this we get the idea of a regime of establishing or determining rights in accordance with law.

According to Plato, justice is the supreme virtue which harmonizes all other virtues. But he conceived that individual virtues were reproductions of the virtues of the state which he identified with the social whole. Hence the nature of justice was to be discovered by examining the harmony of the state. Accordingly, justice consisted in each individual's doing the task appointed to him by the need of maintaining the social order. He must be and must act as a particular organ in the entire body of organized society. Thus in Plato's ideal state the individual is not to find his own level for himself by free competition with his fellows, but every member of the community must be assigned to

JUSTICE ACCORDING TO LAW

the class for which he proves himself best fitted so that a perfect harmony and unity will characterize both the state and every person in it. He had no use for the universal genius who through wisdom was able to become everything and imitate everything. If such a person came to his ideal city he was to be told there were no such there or allowed to be there and he was to be sent to some other city. No one who could not be kept to his assigned place was to be tolerated. In the ideal state justice was the perfect harmony of the whole brought about by everyone, that is each part, doing its own work and abstaining from interfering with its neighbors. The nature of justice in detail depended at bottom on the due assignment of function to each item in the social whole.

Aristotle distinguished universal justice, regard for laws and requirements of life in society generally, which was complete virtue, from particular justice, a special kind of virtue characterized by regard for equality. In this category he distinguished distributive justice from corrective justice, which was called for where a defect in the original distribution had to be righted. The important feature, therefore, was the doctrine of distributive justice. Here the guiding idea of equality became one of proportion according to merit. He believed that the individual man apart from the state became the "most malignant and dangerous of beasts," so that he could "realize his moral destiny only in the state." Accordingly, rights could exist only between those who were free and equal before the state. Justice demanded a unanimity in which there would be no violation of mutual rights, that is, in which each would keep within his appointed sphere. Law took account in the first instance of relations of inequality, in which individuals are treated in proportion to their worth, and only secondarily of relations of equality. The well-known exhortation of St. Paul in which he calls upon everyone to exert himself to do his duty in the class in which he finds himself placed brings out this idea.

Greek philosophy got beyond the primitive conception of law as a device to keep the peace and put in its place an idea of the law as a device to preserve the social *status quo*, to keep each man in his appointed groove and thus prevent friction with his fellows. Justice was regarded as maintenance of the social status quo and philosophers were busied in planning an ideal society in which everyone was put in the right place, to be kept there thenceforth by the law. We may understand this if we remember the condition of perpetual strife between the oligarchs and the demos in the Greek city-state and the mischiefs brought upon many cities by able, restless, ambitious men.

Subsequent attempts to define justice have been much influenced by Aristotle's analysis. Either the actual social order and the normal expectations to which it gives rise are accepted as the final determinative of rights or they are held to be determined by some ideal, commonly equality, as with nineteenth-century socialists or liberty, as with Kant and nineteenth-century philosophical jurists following him. Sidgwick puts the distinction well. He speaks of "conservative justice," respect for "normal expectations" under the social order as it is, and "ideal justice," respect for the rights (i.e., reasonable expectations) involved in social manhood however that idea may be given content. This is paralleled by a distinction we must make with respect to natural law, the ideal law to which the philosophical jurist holds the positive law, the body of norms, that is, authoritative models or patterns of decisions, should be made to conform. This may be what I have been in the habit of calling "positive natural law," an ideal of the actual law of the time and place made to serve as a critique of that law, or what I have called "natural natural law," a pure ideal of what a body of law ought to be according to some philosophical system. Today we see a like distinction in theories of justice. On the one hand, justice is thought of as respect for the expectations involved in civilized life as we know it in the time and place. On the other hand, it may be thought of as respect for the expectations involved in life in a society in which every human being may live a full and equal social and economic existence. Some such ideal is suggested by movements going on in the law of liability to repair damage.

This connects with the doctrine that justice is a moral idea only. A received ideal or picture of the purpose of social control is an element in the body of authoritative norms or models or patterns of decision which is one meaning of the term "law." But these are norms of administering justice. Also they may be thought of as moral precepts. Thus justice and law are looked on as purely moral ideas. Such was the teaching of the eighteenth-century law-of-nature school of jurists. This confuses the ideal relation among men with the ideal development of individual character. What are faults in morals may or may not manifest themselves in tangible infractions of the ideal relation among men, and so may be out of the sphere of the legal adjustment of relations and ordering of conduct. All the conflicts and overlappings of expectations that the law must resolve are not a mere matter of applying moral precepts. If it were, the task of lawyer and judge would be an easy one. It is far from true that every law or every legal precept is or can be declared or applied morals. Take two problems of a type which have made or are making trouble for courts and judges and law teachers. One of the oldest and best known is that of the tailor who in good faith, thinking it his, takes another's cloth and makes of it a suit of clothes. Who is to own the suit? The two schools of jurists in the classical Roman law held to divergent opinions on different arguments. In Justinian's codification of the Roman law a third view was adopted. The French Civil Code took a different line and the German Civil Code of 1900, which has been much followed in the present century, took a fifth. In Anglo-American law Blackstone announced a rule unlike any of the foregoing. Still another was laid down in earlier American decisions. Judge Cooley in Michigan in 1871 worked out another which has been approved for a generation for certain cases. But the limits of its application are uncertain. Every one of these solutions is distinct and it cannot be said that any of them is wholly satisfactory. Some one must own the suit. It cannot be divided. What makes the question difficult is that no moral precept will decide it.

Again, suppose a professional forger draws a check on the account of a well-known businessman so skillfully that what appears to be his commonly known signature is recognized by everyone. He takes it to a department store, makes some purchases, and tenders the check with his endorsement in payment. The cashier and credit man recognize the signature and know the bank to be that in which the apparent drawer has his account. The forger is given the balance in cash and disappears with the goods and the cash. The check is endorsed by the store company and deposited in its bank which gives credit therefor. It is sent to the clearing house the next day which gives credit therefor to the first bank and sends it for collection to the second bank, the one on which it was drawn. That bank, seeing the well-known signature of a regular depositor with a good balance, pays the amount to the clearing house. At the end of the month, when the canceled checks are sent to the supposed drawer, the forgery is discovered. Who is to bear the loss? It can hardly be divided by four. Some one of the four equally innocent persons must bear the loss. But is any one at fault beyond the forger who is out of reach? What moral precept will decide such a case? When it said that "the bank is only a risk-gatherer and distributor under existing law," have we laid down a moral principle as a solution or have we only established a rule of fixing the incidence of the loss in the absence of such a principle? Yet the courts must do so, and we can do no more than fix a rule on the basis of experience and at least be assured that every such case will be decided to the same effect as every other.

Aristotle held that commutative justice (i.e., the virtue which has for its object to render to everyone as near as may be what belongs to him) was the business of the judge. He was to fix punishments and penalties (and in his time reparations or damages were thought of in terms of penalty) equally to all according to the rule of law. Distributive justice—to each according to his merits or deserts—was the business of the legislator. Political rights and the material goods of existence were to be distributed according to distributive justice. But each was to be judged equally with his fellow men. The laws were to have equal application in the courts. On the other hand, the wants, demands, expectations of each were to be satisfied according to what he deserved; according to what he achieved toward his task in society and the value of that task to society. This has been thought a moral proposition. But today it is urged as a moral proposition that courts are to apply the principle of commutative justice (i.e., to bring about equality between the parties so that no one shall be gainer by another's loss) to what Aristotle would have put as a distributive problem of shifting the burden of loss. A radical reconstruction of moral ideas is required to put shifting of the burden of loss to the person most able to bear it, for example, putting the loss in the case of the forged check on the bank with the most capital and surplus or upon the supposed drawer of the check on the ground

JUSTICE ACCORDING TO LAW

that his greater means make the loss relatively light to him. Certainly natural law as a universal moral system of precepts helps us little, if at all, upon questions of adjustment and even compromise of conflicting expectations which arise continually.

An example may be seen in a change as to liability to answer for loss or damage incurred by others. Looking back on the development of the law on this subject in each of the legal systems of the modern world we can see a succession of five ideas as to the basis of such liability. At first there is a simple idea of causation, in its original form the vengeance idea. The beginnings of law asked simply, did the defendant do the physical act which damaged the plaintiff? If he did he aroused in the injured person a desire for vengeance which would lead to private war and disturbance of the peace of society. One who thus endangered the general security must buy off the desire for vengeance he had awakened. Second, there comes in the idea of fault, of culpable causation, a moral idea. This substituted the general morals for the general security as the underlying idea. "The law of to-day," said Dean Ames in 1908, "except in certain cases based upon public policy, asks the further question, 'Was the act blameworthy?' The ethical standard of reasonable conduct has replaced the unmoral standard of acting at one's peril." Third, there came to be an idea of control of the causing factor as determinative of liability to repair loss or damage, a return to the idea of a basis in the general security. Ames noted this in 1908. He said that the basis was blameworthy action except in certain cases "based upon public policy." The public policy to which he referred was the social interest in the general security which called for holding men without regard to fault where they maintained things or employed agencies likely in ordinary experience to get out of hand and do damage, unless at their peril of answering for resulting damage they restrained those things and agencies and kept them within bounds. Cases of liability without fault within this category have steadily multiplied in the present century. Also liability for wrongs done by agents and servants, which covered up liability without fault by a fiction of representation, identifying servant with master and agent with principal, has had a long and detailed development. In the present century an idea came in that liability should be imposed upon those able to pass the loss on to the public—the so-called insurance idea. We were all to bear the losses falling upon any of us as risks of life in civilized society, and, as means of achieving that just distribution of the burden of loss, the law should impose the loss in the first instance upon those able to pass it on to the public at large through charges for services in the case of public utilities, or price of goods manufactured in case of products of the factory, or prices for products raised in agriculture. Lastly, parallel with or else out of the so-called insurance idea a new basis of liability has been increasingly advocated in recent years and is making headway. It looks like an idea of greater ability to bear the loss as a ground of liability.

Thus a shift from the idea of liability as attached to

JUSTICE ACCORDING TO LAW

fault to some newer basis of liability not based on morals nor primarily upon the general security has been going on throughout the world. Sometimes we are told frankly that liability is imposed on one "because the law can find no one else to bear the burden." Sometimes we are told that the basis of liability is not the fault of a wrongdoer but is such a method of distributing the burden of loss "as social policy dictates." A recent writer tells us that there is increasing tendency to shift the emphasis "from moral blame to social responsibility." It might be put as a moral duty of those of greater means to come to the assistance of those of lesser means. But how much greater must the means be to create this duty and how, among those of greater means, is the one who is to bear the loss to be selected?

According to the insurance theory the loss is to fall on one who is in a position to pass it on to all of us. But in the bureau organization of the service state today the proposition as to passing damages for losses incurred by no one's fault on to the public by way of employer or public utility or industrial enterprise is fallacious. One bureau or commission fixed rates for services. Another fixed or may be fixing prices. Another has large control over wages and hours. A jury or some administrative agency fixes responsibility and assesses the damages or the amount of accident compensation. Each of these agencies operates independently, subject to no effective coordinating power. Those that control rates and prices are zealous to keep the cost to the public as low as may be. Those that control the imposition of liability on employers are apt to be zealous to afford the maximum of relief to the insured or to their dependents. With continual pressure upon industry and enterprise to relieve the tax-paying public of the heavy burdens our recent humanitarian programs involve, the practical result is likely to be that the burden is shifted arbitrarily to the most convenient victim. There is little if any reality in the proposition that compensation for loss or injury without fault of the utility or enterprise is passed on to the public.

But the deceptive doctrine that we are all of us insuring each of us by imposing loss and damage on an involuntary Good Samaritan makes for growing acceptance of absolute liability. One of the outstanding state judges of today has proposed extending it to manufactured articles and a state court now seems to have accepted the proposition. Also it is proposed to incorporate it in the new commercial code in preparation by the Commissioners on Uniform State Laws and the American Law Institute. Furthermore a teacher in one of the great law schools of the country argues for abolition of the doctrine of the independent contractor in the law of agency. As the law stands one who employs another to act is liable for fault of the one employed where there is right and power of control over the person immediately acting. Where the actor is an independent contractor there is no such control. But frequently the independent contractor has no means sufficient to be reached on execution. Hence, we are told, losses and injuries are left unrepaired, which must not be. In the same spirit a judge of one of our most important courts intimates that the requirement that one who is required to repair a loss must have caused it is artificial and should be abrogated. See what this means. Suppose X determines to commit suicide but wishes to provide for his dependents. He stands at the corner waiting for a bus or heavy truck as the chosen agent of self-destruction. When one comes along he throws himself beneath its wheels and is killed. If causation and fault as prerequisites of liability are eliminated must not the transportation company or trucking company repair the loss to the widow and children? Thus we achieve high humanitarian purposes by the easy method of using the involuntary Good Samaritan as the Greek playwright used the god from the machine. It may be that we shall call this justice. But the morals are those of Robin Hood or of the pickpocket who was so moved by the eloquence of the preacher of the charity sermon that he picked the pockets of everyone in reach and put the contents in the plate.

For justice as we seek to administer it in the courts we must take account of more than is given us by morals or by natural law.

Maritain says: "The only practical knowledge all men have naturally and infallibly in common is that we must do good and avoid evil. . . . Natural law is the ensemble of things to do and not to do which follow in necessary fashion from the simple fact that man is man, nothing else being taken into account." But all men, in urging their claims and expectations in competition with their fellow

WHAT IS JUSTICE?

men, have been far from able to agree on important details of what is good and what is evil. Each side of many a bitter controversy argues with assurance that its case rests upon eternal principles of right and justice. Each identifies its claims with unchallengeable dictates of morals. If nothing else the everyday discussions between employers and employees would convince us that this sort of natural law can do very little for the lawyer. It is because there is no "natural" guide to solution of so many of these conflicts and overlappings of competing claims and expectations that we must have positive law or go back to private war.

Let me illustrate by a situation of frequent occurrence when I came to the bar in 1890. It was a great advantage to a farmer to get his wheat to an elevator ahead of his neighbors. The first comers for a while got a better price. Hence it was an advantage to have one's own threshing machine to put to work as soon as the crop was gathered in instead of having to wait for a crew of threshers to come around with their machine. But threshing machines cost money and few could afford them. So three or four neighbors would club together and buy one to be owned in common. Three or four could own at the same time but they could not all use at the same time. One of them would get hold of the machine when all four were ready and wanted to use it and some had to wait and lose the advantage of getting to the elevator early. The result was sometimes violence and often litigation, and the law could not do much more than sell the machine and divide the proceeds. Needless to say this satisfied no one.

JUSTICE ACCORDING TO LAW

If we cannot be satisfied with the idea of justice as an individual virtue or with the natural-law theory of justice as morals, shall we say that by justice we mean a regime of social control, as when we speak of the administration of justice?

Such a regime is a necessity of civilized society. Divergent drives of individuals, the frictions inherent in human nature, have to be held down. Indeed, civilization on one side is said to be a conquest of human nature, as on another side it is a conquest of external nature when men are set free to investigate and study and invent. Unless this conquest of human nature is achieved a group dissolves or is disrupted. To achieve it is the task of social control. All of that task, however, is not done by the specialized regime, the legal order, or law in one sense of that term. There are other direct agencies, such as kin-groups in one stage of development of civilization and religious organizations. There are also indirect agencies, addressed immediately to other tasks, which operate more or less effectively to eliminate friction and thus supplement the legal order of a politically organized society. One thinks at once of civic societies, of professional and trade associations, and of social clubs, with their canons of ethics, internal discipline, and traditions of the conduct of a gentleman. But since the sixteenth century politically organized society has been the paramount agency subjecting the coercive action of all others to scrutiny and limiting their regulatory activities. It is not merely that conflicting claims to particular things, such as the suit of clothes made innocently from another man's cloth, or the immediate use of the threshing machine owned in common, or the incidence of loss because of the forged check, cause discord in varying degrees. As experience enables us to straighten out these conflicts new demands and new expectations arise and press upon the legal order persistently until we learn how to do something about them. Since I came to the bar I have seen the claim of the individual laborer to a vested right in the job, as something more than a contract relation, broken if there was a strike, become recognized as legally secured. A new branch of the law has arisen in this way. But there is a task of preventing as well as one of settling such conflicts. Conduct has to be channeled, habit and expectation have to be molded so as to avoid or reduce the development of conflict, as new situations of fact raise divergent expectations. Above all there has to be a system determining who shall decide, who may call for decision, on what basis decision shall be made, and how it shall be carried into effect. When, as in Greece, in Roman law, and in the Middle Ages, orderly maintenance of the social status quo is held to be the end or purpose of social control, justice is taken to be "recognition and observance of the requirements incidental to social status and of those prescribed by custom." These, however, are not constant. As they change new expectations arise and bring about new conflicts.

For example, a heated controversy has arisen in one of the great universities of the land, where college fraternities are allowed space on which to build and maintain chapter houses, whether a fraternity may be recognized if its members claim to choose agreeable associates to live with them while students who belong to racial groups assert what they consider a reasonable expectation of being chosen by socially prominent societies. It is because of the many cases of daily occurrence which do not admit of solution with reference to requirements of social status or custom that we must have a body of authoritative guides to decision. We cannot leave decision to arguable divergent views of morals. But we cannot dispose of all such conflicts by exercise of the force of politically organized society. Much has to be left to other agencies of social control as beyond the limits of effective legal action.

Thinking of justice as a regime of social control established to make law in the sense of a body of ideal norms of conduct effective in action, it has been said to be the "most faithful realization of law." But this puts the cart before the horse. The regime is not established to enforce law as the body of authoritative precepts. Those precepts are established to make the regime of adjustment of relations and ordering of conduct systematic and orderly; to make it operate equally and reasonably so as not to generate further friction. Thus we get back to Aristotle's doctrine that commutative justice is the business of the judge.

Lord Acton proposed to amend Dr. Johnson's saying that the Devil was the first Whig. Instead, Lord Acton held, Thomas Aquinas was the first Whig. He took the first step toward secularizing the idea of justice which in the patristic theory had been a purely theological idea. In developing Aristotle's analysis he took commutative justice to

WHAT IS JUSTICE?

be the justice of contracts and exchange where an idea of equivalents answered to Aristotle's characteristic of equality. Distributive justice was the setting up of a commanding power superimposing itself upon the community. This regime of justice had behind it natural law, human reason which partakes of divine reason, and the eternal law (*lex aeterna*)—the reason of divine wisdom governing the universe. But the regime is not justice. Justice is rather in the natural law and the eternal law behind the regime. But is it in reason itself, which is to govern the regime in action, or shall we say that the regime, governed and directed by reason, is set up to do justice, so that we are to identify justice with the end or purposes of social control and so of law? What is that end or purpose?

To my mind Radbruch, the foremost philosopher of law, as I see it, in the present generation, put the matter best when he defined justice as "the ideal relation among men." We are seeking through social control, and so through that highly specialized form of social control we call law, to bring about and maintain an ideal relation among men. I say "an" ideal relation rather than "the" ideal relation because what is *the* ideal relation, as something ultimate and absolute, is not the settled and no longer debatable question we took it to be in the nineteenth century. At first men took it that the end of law was to keep the peace. Later, as we have seen, Greek philosophers held it was peaceable maintaining of the social status quo, and this idea was accepted in the Middle Ages.

A change begins with the Spanish jurist-theologians of

JUSTICE ACCORDING TO LAW

the sixteenth and beginning of the seventeenth century. Recognizing the facts of the political world of their time, with which the medieval juristic theory of Christendom as an empire was wholly out of accord, they conceived of individual states, and thence ultimately of individual men as equal, since states and men were able to direct themselves to conscious ends and thus their equality was a principle of justice. Holding to an idea of the unity and universality of law as a body of eternal principles, they were led to the conception of restraints by which this equality was maintained and in which it might be expressed. Two types of such restraints suggested themselves, restraints upon states and restraints upon individuals, and these types were taken to be generically one. The restraints upon states, limitations upon their activities which they might not overpass, since they were imposed by eternal principles, might fix the limits of the activities of sovereigns in their relations with each other. Thus these jurists were the forerunners of international law. But these restraints upon states pointed out the limits of the activities of sovereigns in their relations with their subjects, giving us political theory. The restraints upon individuals were considered to have the same basis in eternal principles of universal law and to be of the same nature. They fixed the limits of individual activity in the relations of individuals with each other, giving us juristic theory. Comparing the juristic theory so developed with the juristic theory of antiquity, it will be perceived that the conception of the end of law has undergone a fundamental change. The theory of antiquity thought of the legal order as a limiting of the activities of men in order to keep each in his appointed place and to preserve the social order as it stands. The theory which begins with the Spanish jurist-theologians thinks instead of a limiting of men's activities in the interest of other men's activities because all men have freedom of will and ability to direct themselves to conscious ends and so are equal. Thus instead of a device to maintain a social status quo the legal order begins to be thought of as a device to maintain a natural, i.e., ideal, equality. Out of this developed an idea of justice as liberty; as a condition of maximum free individual self-assertion.

Instead of defining justice some today seek a theory of values by which to measure competing, conflicting, or overlapping expectations. But it may be suggested that this theory of values will give us the ideal relation among men as one in which the theory is fully realized. Moreover, two things further have to be remarked as to referring values to a theory of justice. One is that the ideal relation among men is not all that we have to consider in connection with the end or purpose of law or the ideal element in law in the sense of the body of authoritative precepts in accordance with which the legal order is maintained. Redbruch holds that justice in the sense of the ideal relation among men, morals in the sense of the ideal development of individual character, and security in the sense of assuring men freedom from aggression by others and good faith on the part of others in the general intercourse of society, are in irreducible antinomy. Any one carried out to its full logical development negates the others. We cannot look exclusively

JUSTICE ACCORDING TO LAW

at any one without impairing the others nor can we unify the three in one idea. For example: Criminal law and criminal procedure are embarrassed by an inherent difficulty of achieving some balance or compromise between security and the ideal relation among men. If we look only to security, detection of offenders stands out as of primary importance. We seek maximum effectiveness of criminal investigation. Hence such things as the third degree, extortion of confessions, wire tapping, searches and seizures without warrant, invasion of dwellings in search of evidence, and pretended holdups by detectives disguised as bandits in order to reach documents carried on the person are regarded as legitimate. Criminal investigation in France has leaned in this direction. On the other hand, if we look only at the ideal relation among men or only at the ideal development of individual character such things are abhorrent. Criminal investigation is rigidly limited by bills of rights and we may easily carry this so far as to hamper effective detection and enable many offenders to escape. In general Anglo-American criminal procedure has leaned heavily in this direction. In legal history there has been much swinging back and forth between extreme on the one side and extreme on the other and a wholly satisfactory practical compromise has yet to be found.

A second point is that a satisfactory theoretical solution may prove impossible. It is now held by many that an ultimate theory of values cannot be found. We are told that it is unscientific to seek to formulate values. They are held to be purely subjective. Objective valuations cannot be reached. I dislike to surrender to this give-it-up philosophy. For this way of thinking is nothing new. Postwar theories of futility have been common enough. After Greece had been disrupted by the Peloponnesian War and the wars of the successors of Alexander, Pyrrho taught that agreement was in the nature of things impossible. The wise man must be imperturbable. He could not expect to convince others nor to make assured decisions. Epicurus taught that wisdom dictated inactivity. One could not reach an assured conclusion as to the political controversies of the time and should simply lie low and let things work themselves out. If he was inconspicuous a tyrant would not notice him and he could live serenely. After the first World War skeptical neo-Kantians taught much the same doctrine. But it is significant that experience of totalitarian government convinced Radbruch that he must modify his teaching. There did seem to be certain fundamental expectations involved in life in civilized society which must be recognized and secured if there is to be any real law. St. Augustine relied on religion here. The church was to secure those expectations. Government, which in the disturbed conditions of the breakdown of the Western Roman Empire did not, was a deeply rooted brigandage. The state was no wise different from an association of bandits.

In the further development of political and juristic theory of justice after the Spanish jurist-theologians, the seventeenth and eighteenth century law-of-nature school was of two types: One individualist, the other universal and in a sense socialist. In the former, which had the greater influ-

JUSTICE ACCORDING TO LAW

ence, we may put Hobbes, Pufendorf, Locke, and Kant, who mark the end of that school and the beginning of the nineteenth-century metaphysical school. In the latter, we may put Grotius, Leibniz, and Wolff. Both schools were rationalist and secular. But they held to different theories of justice. In the first type Hobbes and Pufendorf identified justice with the will of the state, while Locke, Rousseau, and Kant after them found justice in a synthesis of liberty and equality. Men, they held, were born free and equal. Justice could be realized only by deducing social control through politically organized society from a postulated pact guaranteeing this innate liberty and equality. Kant separated justice and morals (as we have seen the neo-Kantian Radbruch does today). He confined justice to the governing of the external activity of men and morals to the development of the inner life. To him justice was the external liberty of each limited by the like liberty of all others. Thus the end or purpose of law was promotion and maintenance of the maximum individual free self-assertion. The Kantian idea of justice, the liberty of each adjusted to the like liberty of all others, was received as the ideal relation among men by the jurists of the nineteenth century; but each school arrived at it in its own way and put it in the terminology of its own system.

Nineteenth-century metaphysical jurisprudence was thoroughly abstract individualist. It postulated that the end of man was freedom. It developed the idea of free will into the practical consequence of civil liberty. Hence the end of law was to secure to each individual the widest possible individual liberty. Law as a restraint on individual abstract liberty had to be justified. The justification was that there is no true liberty, i.e., abstract universal liberty, except where there is adjustment of relations and ordering of conduct by systematic application of the force of a politically organized society. Thus the strong are restrained who would interfere with the freedom of action of the weak and the organized many who would interfere with the free individual self-assertion of the few. The test of just law was the amount of abstract individual liberty secured.

While the metaphysical jurists were deducing the whole system of rights and the idea of the purpose of the legal order from a metaphysical conception of free will, the utilitarians sought a practical principle of lawmaking. They were a school of legislators. Their leader, Bentham, did not question abstract individualism. He assumed that the greatest general happiness was to be procured through the greatest individual free self-assertion. His program was, unshackle men; allow them to act as freely as possible. Hence the end of law came to the same thing with him as with the metaphysical jurists.

Nineteenth-century historical jurists were more concerned with the nature of law and the development of the content of legal systems. They took their philosophical ideas from the metaphysical school and so agreed in holding abstract individual liberty to be the fundamental idea. They conceived that the history of law was a story of the realizing or unfolding of the idea of liberty. As Sir Henry Maine put it, the growth of law had been a progress from status to contract. It was a progress from institutions where legally recognized claims and legally imposed duties flowed from a condition in which one was put or in which he found himself without reference to his will and from which he could not divest himself by any manifestation of his will. It was a progress to institutions where rights, duties, and liabilities result from voluntary action, flow from exertion of the will. This movement from status to contract was taken to be the clue to social, political, and legal development.

Somewhat later the doctrines as to the end of law which had become fixed in Anglo-American juristic thought under the influence of the utilitarians and the historical jurists were reinforced in America by the influence of the positivists. Spencer's writings, culminating in his *Justice* (1891) had much vogue. The purpose of the positivist jurists was to find by observation laws of morals, laws of social evolution, and laws of legal development analogous to gravitation, conservation of energy, and the like. But observation led them to the same result to which metaphysics had led the philosophical jurists and history had led the historical jurists. Spencer seems to have thought of the progress from status to contract as the rational outcome of the universe. Abstract freedom of contract was the ideal to which evolution constantly tended. Spencer's formula of justice is substantially Kant's.

Juristic radicalism in the nineteenth century took two paths. On the one hand, the idea of justice as the maximum of individual self-assertion and the prevailing belief that the inevitable realizing of the idea of liberty made conscious, deliberate lawmaking futile led some (the anarchist individualists or philosophical anarchists) to develop to its extreme logical consequences the doctrine that law is intrinsically evil in that it restrains liberty. Hence they advocated a regime of individual action by voluntary cooperation free from coercion by state-imposed rules. On the other hand, the idea of law and government as a means of achieving individual liberty (rather than of leaving it to achieve itself) was taken up by another group which, rejecting political and juristic pessimism but holding to the idea of individual self-assertion as the end, developed what may fairly be called a social individualism. Where the main current of nineteenth-century juristic thought, following the seventeenth and eighteenth-century tradition, opposed society and the individual and was troubled to reconcile government and liberty, this group sought individual liberty through collective action and called for the maximum of governmental control as the means to a maximum of liberty. On another side, in contributing to theories of the social interest in the individual life and in developing the Hegelian idea of the culture-state as distinguished from the Kantian law-state, the nineteenth-century socialists mark the beginnings of a transition to a new conception of the end of law. But in the last century no school questioned that individual liberty was the end.

In a new direction we go back to Grotius, Leibniz, and others following them who thought of society as the cooperation of beings endowed with reason. Society resolved the conflict between the individual and the universal. It brought about a synthesis of the whole and its parts. In such a theory of justice every community and association and group is an agency for promoting justice. It is in the line of recent sociological thinking. Movement in this direction has led to a number of twentieth-century schools which we speak of today as social-philosophical. At the beginning of the century Neo-Hegelians, seeing as the end of law the maintaining, furthering, and transmitting of civilization, were especially active and seemed to promise much. At present there is a revival of natural law, especially in the form of Neo-Scholasticism or Neo-Thomism, which would give us a theory of the end of law by logical deduction from what is given us by revelation and by intelligence, by a technique of choice guided by "the predetermined ends of the legal order which suggest the means of their own realization." It is significant that some outstanding recent French jurists have shifted from Comtian positivism to Neo-Scholasticism without, however, it must be confessed, much change in the substance of their doctrine.

It seems possible to put as the end of law from any of these standpoints the maintaining of an ideal relation among men. But what is that relation? It has been thought of as peace and order, as a secured stable social status quo, as liberty, i.e., a maximum of free individual self-assertion appropriate to a world of opportunities awaiting exploration and exploitation, of a maximum of economic production (Duguit), as a maximum satisfaction of individual expectations, and as a maximum development of human control over external or physical nature made possible by a maximum control over internal or human nature—in other words, of civilization. Today with the rise of the service state we get a new meaning of "security" and an ideal of using the power of politically organized society to deliver mankind from want and fear and frustration. But here we encounter the serious question of what may be done by applying the force of politically organized society to adjustment of relations and ordering of conduct; of the limits of effective legal action and what must be left to other agencies of social control.

At any rate, lawyers are not required to conduct a sitdown strike until philosophers agree, if they ever do, upon a theory of values or a definition of justice. Experience developed by reason and reason tested by experience have taught us how to go far toward achieving a practical task of enabling men to live together in politically organized communities in civilized society with the guidance of a working idea even if that working idea is not metaphysically or logically or ethically convincingly ideal.

What the law has been trying to do is to adjust relations and order conduct so as to give the most effect to the whole scheme of expectations of men in civilized society with a minimum of friction and waste. Often the best that it has proved able to do is to work out a rough compromise between conflicting expectations urged in good faith and confident belief in their intrinsic rightfulness by strong groups or insistent individuals. Dicey pointed this out long ago in the law of libel, and broadcasting and television are

JUSTICE ACCORDING TO LAW

emphasizing it. An example may be seen in the law as to interference by newspaper articles with the due course of criminal trials. In the same way we have found by hard experience that in labor disputes some tolerance of disorder is a practical necessity even where logic would call for strict application of settled rules of law. But it does not follow that our only resource is arbitrary expression of a lawmaker's will on the one hand, or arbitrary determination by some administrative agency on the other hand.

We may come near, for practical purposes, to systematic adjustments and reasoned orderings according to an authoritative technique. I have called this process one of social engineering. The science of law is a science of social engineering having to do with that part of the whole field which may be achieved by the ordering of human relations through the action of politically organized society.

William James tells us that there is a continual search for the more inclusive order. This is illustrated by the history of ideas as to the end of law. Thinkers have continually gone behind an idea of the past to a more inclusive one. As I have said, at first they thought of the end as keeping the peace. But why keep the peace? It seemed to be for the purpose of maintaining the social order. Hence the end was taken to be orderly maintaining of the social status quo. But why maintain the social order? Because to do that makes division of labor possible and so sets us free to exert our natural faculties—to do things. Hence the end was held to be promoting the maximum of free self-assertion. Yet why leave us free to do things? Because freedom to do things is a strong human desire or want or demand. But men want some things, urge some strong expectations, which are not attainable in a regime of maximum free doing of things. Men wish to be free but they want much besides. Thus we come to an idea of a maximum satisfaction of human wants or expectations. What we have to do in social control, and so in law, is to reconcile and adjust these desires or wants or expectations, so far as we can, so as to secure as much of the totality of them as we can. Down to the present that is the more inclusive order.

PART 2

What Is Law?

At the outset it may be asked why do we need law? Cannot social control be carried on and achieve its purposes by an administrative process without lawyer's law, i.e., without an elaborate body of authoritative grounds of or guides to decision? Conceivably it can. There are four theoretical possibilities. There may be administration of justice by the unguided, unchecked will of a ruler or of a magistrate. Such was the justice administered by Harun al-Raschid. But it will be remembered that when

WHAT IS LAW?

he walked the streets of Baghdad in disguise at night, combining relief of the tedium of royal existence with judging malefactors, one wrongdoer who told a clever story would go free while the severest penalty was inflicted on another who to a lesser offence added the heinous crime of boring the Commander of the Faithful. Another example was administration of justice by the king in person in the Middle Ages, and one thinks at once of Louis IX under the oak at Vincennes and Henry II in the Great Hall at Westminster. But Louis IX was a saint and Henry II was by instinct a lawyer. Moreover, when arguments were suggested to Henry which did not suit his policies he put the clerk who suggested them out of court. There are remnants of this direct application of will to the solution of controversies in modern states, notably in legislative justice. That, however, has proved so arbitrary, capricious, and unequal that it is being given up everywhere. In any complex social order, in any highly developed economic order, adjudication cannot operate uniformly, equally, and predictably except in accordance with authoritative models or patterns of determination and an authoritative technique of developing from them the grounds of decision. Moreover, it is a fundamental expectation of life in civilized society that one man's will will not be subjected to the arbitrary will of another. So-called administration of justice in totalitarian states in recent times has shown vividly how the role of law goes further than the social and economic order. It extends to the social interest in the individual life.

An example of the part which authoritative guides to

decision play in adjudication may be seen in a case which occurred in an oriental country in which decision was in part governed by the common law. A law prescribed penalties for passing for a certain distance in front of a religious procession or making noises along the line of such a procession. Another provision in the law gave the right of way to a fire company responding to an alarm of fire. It happened that a religious procession was moving on a street and at the same time a fire company, responding to an alarm, was proceeding on a cross street toward the intersection. The fire company, clanging bells and sounding sirens, sought to cross immediately and within the prohibited distance ahead of the procession. As the neighborhood was one in which religious animosities were acute and the firemen and those in the procession adhered to different faiths, outraged partisans of the procession sought to overturn a hose wagon. They were prosecuted at the instance of adherents of the rival sect, while the firemen were prosecuted at the instance of adherents of the sect whose procession was interfered with. Each relied upon a section of the law. For the fire company it was argued that the public safety was the highest law and hence that the section giving it the right of way should prevail. For those who had sought to vindicate the claims of the procession it was argued that duty to God was the supreme concern to which all else should give way. A way out was found in a rule of the English common law that where there are repugnant provisions in a statute the one last in order shall be taken as the last expression of the legislative will and shall govern. On this basis the firemen prevailed. Here it was necessary to have an authoritative ground of decision which both parties could accept without derogation from their dignity. Reason tested by experience and experience developed by reason give us solutions of such cases where otherwise the wisdom of Solomon would scarcely suffice.

But is law in the lawyer's sense of a body of authoritative grounds or patterns of decision a reality? Does it in reality achieve what it purports to do? There are those who tell us that we postulate an ultimate political power and all derives from it. Constitutional limitations are a contradiction in terms. A democracy must be an absolute rule of a majority through the officials it sets up. A science, it is said, does not trouble itself about subjective ideas of balance and of guaranteed liberties and rights. Rights are no more than inferences from exercise by state officials of the force of a politically organized society. Law is no more than what those officials do. Others tell us that law in the lawyer's sense is an illusion or superstition. Some characterize it as a hypocritical covering up of the brutal self-assertion of a dominant social or economic class. Others assert it is a camouflage of reason covering up the individual personal prejudices or wishes of those who for the time being wield the authority of a politically organized society. Such, we are told, is reality. To postulate anything more behind the single item of judicial or administrative activity is either delusion or fraudulent misrepresentation. The neo-realists, as Cardozo calls them, argue that a regime of adjudication by a magistrate or a deciding agency according to a body of rules attaching definite detailed legal consequences to definite detailed states of fact, or a regime of decision according to a body of authoritative grounds or patterns of decision admitting of adjustment in their application to circumstances of particular cases and of times and places are equally psychologically impossible because human judges cannot keep purely subjective factors from influencing and indeed determining their action. But experience has shown that judges can by trying do a great deal at least of what the law expects of them, and by striving for objective decision as an ideal can come close enough to objective decision for practical purposes even if theoretically they cannot attain it 100 per cent. Einstein has demonstrated that we live in a curved universe in which there are no straight lines or planes or right angles. But we do not on that account discard surveying. The postulates of geometry are sufficiently close to reality on a surveying scale for the practical purposes of a practical activity.

If jurists of the last century somewhat exaggerated the regularity and predictability of the course of judicial decision and the controlling effect of legal precepts upon that course of decision, many jurists of today, not without some warrant in what has been happening recently in a few courts, greatly exaggerate the personal, subjective, arbitrary element therein. The menace in the so-called realist theory in action is that from assuming that we do not in practice attain a high degree of objectivity, or indeed any at all, it leads to an idea that we need not try to attain it and ought not to try to attain it because the attempt would be only pretence. But it assumes an abstract judge sitting alone and takes no account of his training, his having to decide formulated issues which with his decision are public records, and the opinion of the profession by which all that he does is closely scrutinized. It is true that the personality of a judge will affect his interpretation and application of a legal precept to some degree. But he has been trained in the tradition of the law, as have his fellow judges also. From judges steeped in that tradition we may expect to get, and experience shows that we do get, substantially the same technique of reading and interpreting a precept and of applying it. It is chiefly in application of the standard of reasonableness, where the tradition is not clear and settled, and in interpretation of legislation to be applied in the light of new and not clearly defined ideals, that the so-called realist finds the material for his doctrine. To judges well brought up in the common-law tradition the main body of its precepts speak alike no matter what their individual social or economic backgrounds or temperament.

Look, for example, at three great judges of the formative era of American law. Lemuel Shaw was a staunch Federalist, son of a Congregational minister in a small community of farmers and fishermen on Cape Cod. His father was paid mostly in firewood and was very poor. Shaw was a graduate of Harvard, and a schoolteacher and newspaper writer while reading for the bar. In his maturity he lived in the stable commercial environment of Boston of that day. John Bannister Gibson was a Jacksonian Democrat, son of a miller and businessman in a frontier community. What property his father had was all but lost in the depression after the Revolution and his widowed mother had a hard struggle to maintain the family home. In order that her children might be educated she set up and conducted a school. Gibson attended Dickinson College for a time but did not graduate. He practiced law in a developing community and associated with the enterprising builders of frontier society. He evaded baptism and was not active in any church. Thomas Ruffin was a conservative Democrat born and reared on a plantation in Virginia. He was graduated at Princeton. He was by descent and bringing up one of the landed aristocracy of the old South. In his maturity he lived on his own plantation among his fellow gentlemen planters. He was a zealous member of the Episcopal church. Each of these men long dominated the highest court of an important state from which many newer states took their legal traditions and upon whose decisions these newer states built their course of decision. The differences in their parentage, bringing up, social environment, political affiliations, and economic surroundings should, according to the psychological and economic determinists of today, have determined their judicial action decisively and so have led to three different judicial traditions. Yet they cooperated in making a consistent body of law on the basis of the principles of the common law and the technique of applying and developing them which they had been taught in the offices of practicing lawyers, whose apprenticeship ran back to barristers trained in the Inns of Court in England. The judges who have made American law did not find an easy retreat from the hard work of the judicial office in a theory of a psychological impotence of judges to reach impersonal results.

Nor will the realist proposition that there is nothing corresponding to a right going before the legal precept which secures it fare better when we look at what takes place. The theory they propound is that enforcement of claims by politically organized society has taught men to assert claims and demands and expectations, not that the legal order has had to do something about strongly asserted expectations and the law has found by experience what to do. One example which has developed before our eyes will suffice for the present purpose. When I came to the bar in 1890 the relation of employer and employee in industry was purely contractual. One who struck gave up his job and so far as the law went might or might not be hired anew. The law did not teach him to claim a vested right in his job with a contract only to fix wages and hours and such incidents. This generation has seen persistent assertion of that claim at length get full and formal recognition by legislation. The unrecognized claim has become a legal right.

We may assume, then, that law is something actual; that it is not a pretence cloaking what is done by officials, but that officials may act according to law or without law, or against and in violation of law. If so, what does law in the lawyer's sense mean?

There are two words representing two ideas to be found in most languages spoken by peoples among whom law has reached any great development. The one set of words (*ius*, *droit, Recht, diritto, derecho*) has particular reference to the idea of right and justice. The primary notion is ethical. They may mean what is right, or a right, or law. This set of words is used for law in periods of legal history in which law is formative and expanding or developing through juristic writing or some nonimperative agency. The other set of words (*lex, loi, Gesetz, legge, ley*) refers primarily to that which is enacted or set authoritatively, but tends to be used also for law as a whole. This use is appropriate in periods of enacted law and periods of legal history in which the growing point of law is in legislation.

In English the word "right" acquired no more than ethical content. "Law," a word etymologically of the second type, came to be used for the specialized social control through the force of politically organized society. But we make a distinction between "law" and "a law" in which the word is used for a precept set authoritatively by the law-making organ of the state.

These two words, of which the Latin *ius* and *lex* are respectively the types, represent ideas between which definitions of law have moved back and forth in the history of the science of law according to the circumstances of legal systems and the agencies by which their precepts have been formulated for the time being. It comes to a question of putting the stress on one or the other of two elements in the legal system—of whether to emphasize rule or discretion. This is one of the persistent problems of the science of law.

WHAT IS LAW?

That problem is too large to be discussed here. It is enough to suggest that inheritance and succession to estates of deceased owners, interests in property and the conveyance thereof, matters of commercial law, and the creation, incidents, and transmission of obligation, with respect to which the social interest in the security of transactions is especially strong, have proved at all times a fruitful field for effective legislation. But where the questions are not of interests of substance, where they do not immediately affect the economic order, but are questions of weighing of human conduct and passing upon its moral aspects, legislation has accomplished little. No codification of the law of torts (wrongs) has achieved any notable measure of success. Indeed, modern codes on this subject are content with significantly broad generalizations. It is not an accident that the Anglo-American law of torts has established itself in Louisiana under a French code or that judicial decision has more weight in the law of liability for wrongs than anywhere else in French law. In the United States, where we rely little upon legislation except as declaring and systematizing the results of judicial experience, succession to decedents is everywhere a matter of statutes and no one questions that the statutes operate well. More and more our commercial law is being codified and the law of property, with respect to which in a modern community certainty is an imperative requirement, has been put in legislative form as to estates in land in England and will no doubt afford a like opportunity for uniform legislation in the United States. On the other hand, in those parts of the law where we have to do more than delimit interests of substance and devise means of securing them, not only do we meet with little legislation and that confined to generalizations of little practical utility, but in the administration of our traditional law of judicial or juristic origin, we find it expedient, if not even necessary, to leave a wide margin of discretion, as, for example, in the standard of the reasonable man in our law of negligence and the standard of the good and diligent head of a household applied by the Roman law and especially the modern Roman law to so many questions of fault where the question is really one of good faith. All attempts to cut down this margin by hard and fast rules have proved futile.

As we now see it, the more flexible traditional element, with its greater scope for adjustment and capacity for more rapid growth, may best be used for that part of social control having to do with repairing injuries, whether those attributable to culpable conduct or those for which maintenance of the general security or humanitarian reasons move us to impose liability for reparation regardless of fault. Also it is best adapted to that part of the law having to do with good faith in relations with one's fellow men, which do not admit of complete justice by application of fixed precepts. But it has taken a long course of experience to teach us this. It was long assumed that the whole task of the law was to be done by means of rules or else that it was to be done by discretion. Reaction from rigid rules led to overwide margins for discretion or discretion super-

WHAT IS LAW?

seding rules. Reaction from a regime of substantially unchecked discretion led to return to mechanical application of rules or logical application of authoritative starting points for reasoning. Attempts have been made to define law wholly in terms of the imperative element or wholly in terms of the traditional element. Very generally in the nineteenth century jurists sought to eliminate discretion from the idea of law. There are some today who would eliminate rule. Here as in the definition of justice we have to take account of ideas, either of which carried to its logical extreme negates the other, which nevertheless are equally necessary for achievement of our practical task and must be kept in balance.

The question what is law has been a battleground of legal philosophers ever since the Greeks began to think about such things, at least as long ago as the fourth century B.C. A dialogue attributed to Plato purports to give a discussion and definition by Socrates (B.C. 459–399) which appeals to jurists today. At least it states the controversial views about which we are still arguing. The question is as hotly debated in the modern world as it was in antiquity. Three things have operated to make it a difficult question. One, the need of balance between rule and discretion, has been spoken of. Another is that there are at least four points of view from which law in the lawyer's sense of a body of authoritative precepts may be looked at, and a different view is reached according to the point chosen. A third is that three quite different things have gone by the name of "law" as used by lawyers, and men have often tried to define all

JUSTICE ACCORDING TO LAW

three or some synthesis of them in terms of some one of them.

It is instructive to consider the standpoints from which law in the sense of a body of authoritative precepts may be looked at. First is the standpoint of the lawmaker. He thinks of items of desired conduct, of something he considers ought to be done or ought not to be done, and so of a command emanating from him to do it or not to do it. This was long the way law was looked at and defined by jurists. Today the realist puts the result from this standpoint in terms of a theory of a law as a threat. It is a threat that, given certain conduct or a certain state of facts, those who wield the force of politically organized society will apply that force in a certain way. This defines law in terms of rules, by no means the most significant part of one element in law used in the ordinary sense in which it is used by lawyers.

Another standpoint is that of the individual subject to the precept. He may, no doubt, think of it as a threat. But more commonly from his standpoint it has been thought of as a rule of conduct, a guide telling him how he should act at the crisis of action. This is the oldest idea of a law. It goes back to the codified ethical custom of the earlier stages of legal development.

Still another standpoint is that of the judge called upon to decide a controversy. To him a law is a guide to decision or a model or pattern of decision.

Finally, there is the standpoint of the counsellor or legal adviser. To him a legal precept, especially a principle or a precept defining a legal conception, is a basis of prediction. As it is the function of the judge to decide, it is the function of the counsellor to predict how a controversy arising from the facts submitted to him will be decided and what course the tribunals will take upon a course of action which the client proposes to pursue. From this standpoint Holmes defined a law as a prediction—a prediction of what courts or administrative agencies or officials will do on a given state of facts. In fairness, however, it should be noted that this was propounded in a lecture in a law school in which he was urging the importance of the counsellor's function in the economic order of today and the need that the law schools should hold this aspect of their task well in mind where they had been thinking and teaching with reference to the advocate's function. Because even from the standpoint of the counsellor a law or a legal precept is not a prediction. It is the adviser, not the law, that does the predicting. As Mr. Justice Cardozo pointed out, it is a basis of prediction.

Can the different ideas reached from these four standpoints be unified? I submit that they can. They can be unified in terms of the idea from the standpoint of the judge. Judges and benches of judges are expected to and for most purposes will follow and decide in accordance with the established precept. Hence it can serve as a guide to conduct, as a threat, and as a basis of prediction. This accords with the way in which the law has developed. Although Sir Henry Maine's proposition that the judge precedes the law, that law in the sense of a body of authoritative precepts

JUSTICE ACCORDING TO LAW

grows out of experience and tradition of adjudication of disputes, has been doubted, the studies made by Llewellyn have amply confirmed it. Thus the guide to or model or pattern of decision is historically the original idea.

Two other theories of law from a different standpoint deserve notice. Some today say that law is power, where we used to think of it as restraint upon power. Social control requires power to influence the behavior of men through the pressure of their fellow men. The legal order as a highly specialized form of social control rests upon the power or force of politically organized society. But so far from the law being power, it is something that organizes and systematizes the exercise of power and makes power effective toward the maintaining and furthering of civilization. What the power theory may mean in action has been exemplified in recent times in the identification of international law with power which has been leading to its undoing.

Another theory of a law thinks of it as an authoritative canon of value. Those who urge this conceive that it is impossible to prove any moral principles or precepts or criteria of ought or measure of valuing conflicting or overlapping human demands or expectations. Hence, they tell us, those who wield the force of politically organized society, formulating the self-interest of a socially or economically dominant class, arbitrarily lay down or establish canons of value and constrain the rest of humanity to follow them. But much of what the Roman jurists of the classical era learned from experience as to how to order conduct and adjust relations with a minimum of friction and waste pro-

WHAT IS LAW?

ceeds from a different social order and a differently organized and centralized administration than we know today. Nonetheless the maxims and legal conceptions and precepts they worked out are of everyday application in the law. Socially and economically dominant classes have changed many times since Rome of the first and second centuries. Yet consider how many precepts formulated by the jurisconsults of that time have governed important relations and ruled important types of conduct ever since.

Historical jurists in the nineteenth century and sociologists (as distinct from sociological jurists) today use the term "law" for all social control. But social control is a sufficient term for the whole concept of the control exercised over each of us through the inner order of the groups and associations and relations that make up society and is involved in living with one's fellow men in varying degrees of contact. Since the sixteenth century one form of social control, control through systematic application of the pressure, or if you will the force, of a politically organized society has been paramount and claims a monopoly of exercise of force. Our concern is with that specialized and most highly organized type. Law in the lawyer's sense has to do with that form of social control.

Limiting the term "law" accordingly, there are three meanings given to it by jurists which must be looked into. What I shall try to do is to set them off, analyze the concepts defined, suggest the appropriate name of each, and endeavor to show the practical importance of so doing. For I have little patience with analysis and definition and classification for their own sake. They are useful instruments. But their value is measured not by the originality and ingenuity displayed in working them out but by how far they may be used to understand what is analyzed and defined and how far that understanding may enable us to make them achieve their purpose.

Specifically the three meanings are (1) the legal order, (2) the body of authoritative guides to or models or patterns of decision, whether judicial or administrative, and (3) the judicial process to which today we must add the administrative process.

(1) The legal order, while usually denominated law in the English-speaking world, deserves a name of its own, as it has among Continental jurists. It is a regime of social control—the regime of adjusting relations and ordering conduct by the systematic and orderly application of the force of a politically organized society. This is what we mean when we speak of respect for law, of law and order, and the like. A law-respecting man who has every desire to uphold the regime of the legal order may yet carry his objections to some particular legislative or administrative regulation or some precept of the traditional law to the point of disobedience. Eighteenth-century jurists used to speak of a right of private judgment in such cases. But this can at most be moral. To make of it a legal right, a guaranteed expectation of immunity from the legally appointed consequences of disobedience, would defeat or disrupt the legal order.

(2) The second sense is the one in which lawyers habitu-

WHAT IS LAW?

ally use the term "law." It is the meaning which the word has borne since the classical Roman jurists and the one to which we may well restrict it in the science of law. It is this meaning we have in mind when we speak of the common law or American law or the law of Missouri or comparative law or the law of property or the law of contract. Law in this sense calls for careful analysis to which I shall proceed after looking at the third meaning.

(3) Today many, especially the self-styled realists, apply the term "law" to the process of determining causes and controversies according to the authoritative guides for the purpose of upholding the legal order. If we adhere to the realist doctrine that law in the second sense is mere pretence we may well keep the term for the first meaning, eliminating perhaps the idea of systematic application of force but retaining the idea of orderly application. In this sense law is said to be whatever is done officially. When used in the sense of systematic application to disputes and controversies in accord with the authoritative guides to decision, Mr. Justice Cardozo has happily given to this meaning the name of "the judicial process."

There are, then, these three ideas, and the three ideas, each called by the same name, have done much to confuse discussions of the subject. Definitions have been drawn with exclusive reference to one meaning and then put universally as somehow defining a unit embracing all three.

If the three ideas denoted by the three meanings can be unified it is by the idea of social control. We may think of a regime which is a highly specialized form of social control, carried on in accordance with a body of authoritative precepts, applied in a judicial and in an administrative process. But we can hardly say that the regime, the body of precepts, and the process of applying them to maintain the regime are one. It avoids confusion to think of the regime and the means of maintaining it as distinct, although in the science of law we have to think of them in connection with each other.

Most of the controversy over the nature of law, which was carried on with some heat between analytical, historical, and philosophical jurists in the nineteenth century, was directed to the body of authoritative materials for the determination of controversies. The question was shifted to the legal order at the end of the century by social-philosophical jurists and in the present century the neo-realists, who denied reality of the authoritative precepts, shifted it to the nature of the judicial process. As to the body of authoritative materials for decision of controversies there is here no simple conception. Law in that sense is made up of precepts, technique, and ideals. There is a body of authoritative precepts, developed and applied by an authoritative technique in the light of authoritative traditional ideals.

When we think of law in the second sense we are likely to think only of the body of precepts. But the technique of developing and applying those precepts, the art of the lawyer's craft, is quite as authoritative and no less important. Indeed it is this technique element which serves to distinguish from each other the two great systems of law in the modern world. Some examples will bring this out.

In the common law, the system of law of the English-speaking world, a statute furnishes a rule for the cases within its purview but not a principle, a starting point for reasoning as to cases outside its purview, not a basis for analogical reasoning. For that, in the common-law system, we look to experience of the administration of justice as shown in the reported decisions of the courts. In the civil-law system, the system of the other half of the world which builds upon the Roman law, the technique in this respect is wholly different. The civilian reasons by analogy from legislative precepts and regards a fixed course of judicial decision on some point as establishing that precise point but not as providing a principle. It does not give a starting point for legal reasoning.

This is an important point for understanding what law is. Let me illustrate it. In Roman law in order that one acquire title to an item of property by adverse possession it was necessary that the thing be something in which property could be acquired, that it be held under some title, that it have been taken in good faith, that it have been possessed exclusively and adversely, and that the possession have been continuous for the time fixed by law. The Roman law required some just title, even if bad or defective. The French Civil Code provided instead that in all cases of movables possession should stand for title. A common-law lawyer, English or American, Canadian or Australian, would say: This proposition is laid down in the code in the part having to do with acquisition of title to property by adverse possession. Hence its application must be limited to the situation for which it was there enacted. It is not to be made to apply by analogy in other fields of the law. But the civilian, thinking of legislation as an ascertainment and declaration of a principle, does not hesitate to employ a legislative proposition as a starting point for reasoning anywhere in the law.

How the Anglo-American common law reasons by analogy is illustrated by the letter-of-credit cases which developed after our entry into the first World War in 1917. In the course of manufacture and export under corporations set up by our government and carried on by letters-of-credit, a question arose whether a letter-of-credit could be pledged. On this question recourse was had to an obsolete English practice of equitable mortgage of land by deposit of title deeds which was not received in the United States. In the absence of a system of recording conveyances, an owner of land kept his title deeds and when he sold the land turned the title deeds over as showing what he had to convey. He could not expect to sell the land without producing them. But if he had pledged them he could not get them back to produce to a purchaser until he paid the debt for which they were pledged. Thus the pledgee of the title deeds had control of the disposition of the land. Courts of equity, looking at the substance rather than the form, treated the transaction as equivalent to a mortgage. This analogy was applied to the pledging of letters-of-credit. The pledgor of the letter could not get his money from the purchaser of the manufactured articles without attaching the letter to the bill of lading. He could not get the letter until he paid the debt for which it was pledged. Hence it was held the pledgee of the letter had a lien on the fund. The civilian would not think of reasoning from a course of judicial decision in this way.

Again, it was a settled common-law proposition that the owner of land owned the air space above the surface indefinitely upward; *usque ad coelum,* up to heaven, it was said. When aerial navigation came in the question was raised whether those who flew over another's land were trespassers. This gave the common-law courts no difficulty. The owner of land might own the bed of a stream flowing over his land or if it flowed along his land own the bed to the middle thread of the stream. But the courts had determined that the public could use the stream for boating and fishing. On this analogy the public could use the air space above land for flying airplanes.

To give a second example of difference of technique, in the common-law system substituted relief, a sum of money by way of reparation, is the normal course. Specific relief, giving a complainant the specific thing to which he is entitled or compelling the specific doing of something or specific undoing of what has been done is given only exceptionally when substituted relief, a money equivalent or money damages, is not adequate to secure the right. Take, for example, a contract to transfer a specific block of shares of stock in a particular corporation. With us the ordinary remedy is damages, an amount of money which will buy the agreed number of shares of that stock on the market, or, if they were to be sold, the value of the bargain to the buyer. But in a special case, where it is of real importance actually to have that number of shares of that particular stock and they are closely held and could not be bought on the market, we should give specific relief and require transfer as agreed. In the civil law it is the reverse. The civilian gives specific relief as a rule. But where it is inequitable or impossible to give specific relief he gives substituted relief instead. The technique in each system is no less authoritative than the precepts which it develops and applies.

Third, there is the ideal element, a body of received, authoritative ideals. This element comes at bottom to a picture of the social order of the time and place, a legal tradition as to what that social order is and so as to what is the purpose of social control, which is the authoritative background of interpretation and application of legal precepts and is crucial in new cases in which it is necessary to choose from among equally authoritative starting points for legal reasoning.

Take, for example, a question in the law of torts upon which the English courts and many of our strongest American courts have differed, on which, however, our American courts are not unequally divided, namely, the question of liability without regard to fault where something which one maintains upon his land, which is potentially liable to get out of hand and do damage, although not a nuisance, yet does escape and cause injury to a neighbor's land. Here we have to choose between the general security, calling for an absolute liability, and the individual life, calling for liability only where there has been fault. It has been suggested that the difference between the English conception of land as a permanent family acquisition and an American conception of land as an asset or a place to do things and carry on enterprises; in other words, a different ideal or picture of society has dictated the starting points for reasoning.

Likewise in interpretation the ideal element is decisive. Massachusetts and Missouri have differed in interpreting exactly the same language in statutes doing away with estates tail. The language not being decisive the question got down to one of the intrinsic merit of the possible interpretations. How was that merit determined? Clearly by the ideal in the time and place of what an American social order should be. In New England the perpetuation of a family had a part in that picture which it did not have in the Southwest.

The most familiar cases of the operation of the ideal element, however, are to be seen in the application of standards. Many standards involve an idea of reasonableness. The law enjoins what is reasonable under the circumstances. But there is often no authoritative legal precept telling us that this is reasonable and that is not. One does not require any protracted study of decisions in the last generation on due process of law to see that application of the standard of reasonableness was governed by a received picture of a pioneer, rural, agricultural society, and that a picture of the urban, industrial society of today has been yielding different results.

Nor have we done with the complexities of the subject when we have distinguished the three meanings of the term "law" and the three elements in law in the second sense. For the precept element, which is commonly taken for all that we have to consider, is made up of rules, principles, precepts defining legal conceptions and precepts prescribing standards.

A rule is a precept attaching a definite detailed legal consequence to a definite detailed state of facts. It is the earliest type of legal precept and primitive law never gets any further. Primitive codes are made up of such precepts. For example, in the Code of Hammurabi, "If a free man strike a free man he shall pay ten shekels of silver"; in the Salic law, "If anyone shall have called another 'fox' he shall be condemned to three shillings"; in the Roman Twelve Tables, "If the father sell the son three times, let the son be free from the father." Criminal codes are made up in greatest part of precepts of this sort. They are to be found chiefly today in the law of inheritance and succession, in the law of property, and in some parts of commercial law. But as experience shows the impossibility of providing in this way for every conceivable detailed state of facts a great forward step is taken in the formulation of legal principles.

A principle is an authoritative starting point for legal reasoning. Principles are the work of lawyers, organizing judicial experience by differentiating cases and putting a reason behind the difference and by comparing a long developed experience of decision in some field, referring some cases to one general starting point for reasoning and yet others to some other such starting point, or finding a more inclusive starting point for a whole field.

Consider such principles as that where one intentionally does something which on its face is an injury to another he must respond for the resulting injury unless he can justify it, or that one who culpably causes injury to another by subjecting him to an unreasonable risk will be held liable for the injury, or that one person is not to be unjustly enriched at the expense of another. In none of these is there any definite detailed state of facts presupposed and no definite detailed consequences attached. Yet we turn continually to such starting points for reasoning and make them the foundation of new departments of the law.

Or consider how starting from a principle as to the duty of a common carrier the precepts worked out for the carter were extended in one line to the stage coach, to the railroad, to the trolley line, to the auto truck, to the airplane, without having to devise new rules as one type of carrier succeeded another. Consider how in another line they were extended to telegraph, telephone, radio, gas for lighting and natural gas for heating, electric light and power. Then note how lawyers worked out a broader principle as to duties involved in a public service which has enabled our law to deal with one after another of these rapidly developing agencies of public service by affording a starting point for reasoning.

JUSTICE ACCORDING TO LAW

A legal conception is an authoritative category into which cases may be fitted so that, when placed in the proper pigeonhole, a series of rules and principles and standards become applicable. Examples are sale, bailment, trust. In these cases there is no definite detailed legal consequence attached to a definite detailed state of facts. Nor is there a starting point for reasoning. There are instead defined categories into which cases may be put with the result that certain rules and standards become applicable.

Principles and legal conceptions make it possible to get along with many fewer rules and to deal with assurance with new cases for which no rules are at hand. In Anglo-Saxon law the laws of Ethelbert (about 600 A.D.) in twenty-nine sections prescribe the exact composition for every physical injury to another's person, going into the greatest detail. If we compare this with a modern text on battery we may see what principles have done for the law.

A standard is a measure of conduct prescribed by law from which one departs at his peril of answering for resulting damage or loss. Examples are the standard of due care not to subject others to unreasonable risk of injury; the standard of reasonable service, reasonable facilities, reasonable rates, imposed upon public utilities; the standard of fair conduct of a fiduciary. There is a characteristic element of fairness or reasonableness in standards which makes them a point of contact between law and morals. This is a source of difficulty. As has been said, there is no precept defining what is reasonable and it would not be reasonable to formulate one. In the end, reasonableness and what is

WHAT IS LAW?

fair have to be referred to conformity to the authoritative ideal.

Conduct requires standards. It is enough to speak of one futile attempt to reduce conduct to rule for purposes of the civil side of the law, namely, the old stop, look, and listen rule as to vehicles crossing railroad tracks. Compare applying this rule to a horse and buggy or farmer's lumber wagon crossing a single track railroad, where trains ran not more than thirty miles an hour, with a long heavy motor truck crossing a four-line track on which streamlined trains as like as not may be going one hundred miles an hour. By the time the driver has stopped, got off the truck, looked up and down the tracks, got back on his truck and started up again, a streamlined train may have come four miles.

But, you may say, why have I gone into all this so much in detail? Has it any practical importance? Most assuredly it has. The greater part of the complaint which the administration of justice has encountered in the present century has grown from the assumption that "law" has one simple meaning; that we can treat it as an aggregate of laws, that a law is a rule and is a simple thing. Treating the standard of due process of law as if it were a rule of property long sorely embarrassed our public law. Every department of the law has been embarrassed by the attempt at a jurisprudence of phrases; by premature formulations of supposed principles. Text writers have often sinned greatly in this connection. The stability of the legal order has been gravely compromised by supposed overrulings which only overruled a text writer or hasty judicial language while the

JUSTICE ACCORDING TO LAW

line of decision remained constant. Law is more than an aggregate of laws. It is what makes laws living instruments of justice. It is what enables courts to administer justice by means of laws; to restrict them by reason where the lawmaker exceeds his reason, and to develop them to the full scope of the reason where the lawmaker falls short of it.

Thinking of law in terms of laws has led to false ideas of our common-law technique and as to our doctrine of precedents. We must remember the relatively short life of rules. Consider the stage coach, the railroad, the motor bus, the airplane. We have not had to make the law over as these changes in the agencies of transportation have succeeded each other. But how many rules applicable to the particular type of conveyance have ceased to be applicable to questions or situations which arise in the courts today. Nevertheless they are not always nor wholly negligible. When air transportation first attracted attention many inferred that legislation would be called for. Yet the common law found no trouble in meeting what was called for. There was a principle at hand from the analogy of the case of owners of the bed of a stream where there is nevertheless a public right of boating and fishing and our law proved to require little beyond administrative adjustment of routes and schedules and facilities.

We must ever bear in mind that in law we have a taught tradition of experience developed by reason and reason tested by experience. One of the significant phenomena in the history of civilization is the vitality of such taught traditions. The civil law is a taught tradition of the Continental

WHAT IS LAW?

universities from the fifth century to the present and connects with another taught tradition of the classical Roman jurisconsults. The common law grew up as a taught tradition in the Inns of Court on the basis of adjudication in the courts. It was a taught tradition handed down from lawyer to apprentice from the seventeenth century, and is now coming to be a taught tradition of academic law schools. Both of the two great legal systems of the modern world are taught traditions and so have proved resistant to forces that destroy political institutions. We have in our law such a tradition molded through the technique of the lawyer to the ever-changing conditions of time and place and so one of the most enduring of human institutions. The last of the Caesars fell three decades or more ago. The work of the jurisconsult contemporaries of the first Caesar still helps guide the administration of justice in half of the world.

Despite the pronouncements of self-styled realists, despite the rise of absolutism in many parts of the world, we may say as Paul did to Timothy, "We know that the law is good, if a man use it lawfully."

PART 3

Judicial Justice

We have asked what is the end or purpose of the legal order, and what is the nature of law by which men seek to maintain that order and achieve its purposes. Now we come to what the skeptical realist argues is actually the whole story—the way in which those who wield the power to apply the force of a politically organized society do in fact employ it toward the adjustment of relations and ordering of conduct, and whether it is possible to have a legal order operating according to law. The so-

JUDICIAL JUSTICE

called realist teaching, for I have always insisted that the word "realist" in this connection is a boast rather than a description, challenges the doctrine of separation of powers, a legal-political doctrine which has been carried furthest in the Constitution of the United States and the constitutions of the several states. We are told that this doctrine, which American lawyers of the last century regarded as fundamental, was a fashion of eighteenth-century thought derived from a forecast made by Aristotle (for there was nothing of the sort in his time) and a mistaken interpretation of the British polity of his time by Montesquieu. We are told, too, that it is outmoded and ought to give way to the exigencies of administration in the service state of today. But it was not without good reason, based on experience, that Americans, almost at the moment independence was declared, began to set up written constitutions and put the separation of powers at their foundation. From the beginning down to the Revolution the colonies had been subjected to a completely centralized government, with no distribution of powers and had learned what that sort of government meant. Ultimately all power over what went on in the colonies was in the King in Council, i.e., the Privy Council. This undifferentiated authority was exercised in the administrative manner. Experience of this form of government led lawyers and statesmen who had read Montesquieu and Blackstone to the express and emphatic pronouncements as to separation of powers which followed on the heels of the Declaration of Independence.

JUSTICE ACCORDING TO LAW

In the nineteenth century philosophical jurists deduced the separation of powers from the idea of liberty and so took it to be a necessary dogma for a state ruled by law. Also an attempt was made to apply sharp analytical lines in applying it. It was assumed that every detailed activity of government must necessarily be once and for all referred to some one department of government. In practice the analytical criterion gave way to a compromise with a historical approach, looking to the powers of Crown, Parliament, and Courts in the English polity before the Revolution. But the difficulties raised by the analytical approach were not obviated, so that well into the present century needed and legitimate conferrings of power upon administrative agencies were held unconstitutional. A solution meeting the practical situation consistently with the Constitution was found by Chief Justice Marshall in 1825, though it did not get general recognition till the present century. There are governmental powers of doubtful classification, which may be held properly to belong to either of more than one department of government. In such cases it is a legislative function to assign the power to one of the appropriate departments. Before this had been generally perceived and while many courts were obstinately insisting that every item of governmental action must be referred exclusively to some one of the three departments provided by the Constitution, there was much and well-justified dissatisfaction with the constitutional doctrine, leading to a strong attack upon this feature of our polity at the beginning of the century which has not ceased since

JUDICIAL JUSTICE

the occasion of it has passed. But recent examples of totalitarian government show what the separation of powers was devised to save us from and I shall assume that our administration of justice will continue to be held to conform to it.

Closely connected with the problem of rule and discretion, of justice according to law and justice without law, is the question by whom justice is to be administered. Is there to be a specialized organ of the state for the performance of the judicial function, or is the function to be performed in whole or in part by organs charged with other functions as well? Is there to be administration of justice by judicial specialists (I call this judicial justice) or by those who exercise other governmental functions as well? If legislative, I call it legislative justice. If administrative, I call it executive justice. Or should the function of adjudication be performed partly by one and partly by the others, and, if so, how and where shall we draw the line?

First, then, as to legislative justice. It died slowly in England, hanging on a long time in legislative divorce, acts of attainder, and bills of pains and penalties, in impeachment, and in private acts of Parliament affording individuals special relief not open to them in the courts. Also until 1844 the appellate jurisdiction of the House of Lords had not clearly set off the House as a court from the House as a legislative body. The turning point was when in the writ of error in the case of the outlawry of O'Connell Lord Lyndhurst persuaded lay peers not to vote. When its appellate jurisdiction was to be exercised only by the law Lords there

JUSTICE ACCORDING TO LAW

was a court where there had been a legislative assembly. Legislative divorce in England came to an end in 1857. Bills of attainder and bills of pains and penalties are regarded as obsolete. The abortive bill of pains and penalties against Queen Caroline (1820) is said to be the last of its kind. Also the impeachment of Lord Melville (1806) is said to be the last.

In the United States legislative divorce existed in the colonies and in many states well after the Revolution; in Rhode Island till 1851, in Pennsylvania till 1874, and as late as 1887 it was held that the legislature of a territory could grant a legislative divorce. In 1888–89 the Alabama legislature granted one, but the courts held it unconstitutional.

Acts of attainder and bills of pains and penalties were common during and after the Revolution. In Rhode Island the legislature had jurisdiction in insolvency till 1832. In Pennsylvania the legislature regularly gave equitable relief till 1837 and could do so till 1874. In Connecticut the legislature administered *cy pres* relief in cases of charitable trusts and even in ordinary trusts till 1877 and exercised supplementary probate jurisdiction during the nineteenth century. For some time after the Revolution a practice obtained in some states of legislative granting of new trials after final judgment in the courts. In Maryland legislation setting aside dismissals for procedural reasons and requiring causes to be continued or heard at certain terms obtained until the last quarter of the nineteenth century. Appellate jurisdiction was exercised by the senate in New

JUDICIAL JUSTICE

York till 1846 and by the legislature in Rhode Island till 1857.

This sort of legislation all but came to an end in the nineteenth century. The federal constitution in 1787 forbade enactment by the states of acts of attainder or bills of pains and penalties. In consequence of constitutional provisions as to separation of powers the courts put an end to legislative granting of new trials early in the nineteenth century by refusing to recognize the acts as valid. About all that is left of legislative justice in the United States is impeachment and legislative adjudication of claims against the state. A better provision as to removal of federal judges, strongly supported, is before Congress superseding impeachment, and the federal government and many states, by providing courts or commissions of claims, have put justice between state and citizen (at least as to contract claims in some jurisdictions) on a footing of law rather than of politics.

Thus by the end of the nineteenth century legislative justice had become substantially obsolete both in England and the United States.

Examining the actual operation of legislative justice in the several cases named, it may be said without hesitation that in action it exhibits all the bad features of justice without law.

In the first place, legislative justice is uncertain, unequal, and capricious. Bills of attainder even in modern times were too often merely legislative lynchings, and bills of pains and penalties, of which there were many examples during and just after the Revolution, were enacted capriciously and were procured on grounds of ill will as well as in the grave cases of danger to the commonwealth for which they were supposed to be reserved and became deservedly odious. In Rhode Island and Connecticut we are told that legislative divorces were sought and granted in cases "too flimsy or too whimsical for judicial treatment."

Again, legislative justice in its relatively short history in this country and in the relatively smaller number of cases in which it was exercised showed the influence of personal solicitation, lobbying, and even corruption far beyond anything charged against our courts by even the most bitter opponent of our judicial system in the course of a long history and after disposition of a huge volume of litigation. In Pennsylvania in the debates in the Constitutional Convention in 1873 which abolished legislative justice in that commonwealth it was brought out that it had become a regular practice for those seeking the legislature rather than the courts for legal relief to employ a member of the legislature as counsel to take charge of the case and put it through. As was said justly in the debate nothing of the sort was ever heard of in purely judicial tribunals.

Third, legislative justice has always proved highly susceptible to the influence of passion and prejudice. This was one of the chief causes of the odium which attached to acts of attainder and bills of pains and penalties at the end of the seventeenth century. It has been especially marked in legislative impeachments. It stood out in the crudely partisan rulings of the Senate on appeals from rulings on

JUDICIAL JUSTICE

questions of evidence or objection by the managers during the impeachment of Andrew Johnson.

Fourth, it has been disfigured everywhere by party politics, partisanship, and often crude "deals" which have been especially characteristic of legislative allowance and disallowance of claims against the state. Experience has shown abundantly that flimsy and even fictitious claims with political backing got allowed while meritorious claims without such backing failed or were put off. It was not merely that disinclination to pay honest claims earned for the doctrine of state immunity from suit the name of the state's prerogative of dishonesty. Claims were allowed on partisan grounds which could not stand the scrutiny of a court for a moment. Hence there has been an increasing tendency in the United States in the present century to turn claims against the government over to judicial tribunals. Legislative investigations are notoriously and often crudely partisan. Finally, legislative justice has been disfigured very generally by a practice of participation in argument and decision by many who had not heard all, or sometimes not even a substantial part, of the evidence and had not heard the arguments of counsel.

Are there any advantages in the administration of justice by legislative bodies to be set over against these serious defects? The one advantage that has been claimed for it is that it is more responsive to the popular will than judicial justice. Likewise in agitation at the beginning of the century for direct popular justice in certain cases the advantage claimed was that justice would be made more im-

JUSTICE ACCORDING TO LAW

mediately and completely expressive of the popular will. The confusion of will and impulse in this claim has been remarked repeatedly. But another consideration is decisive. The psychology of such tribunals is too much and too often the psychology of the crowd or mob. In a court training, long habit, and the critical scrutiny of a learned profession keep down the tendency to throw off individual responsibility, to abdicate individual reason, and to yield to suggestion and impulse. In a large body not so trained and without judicial habits we should expect, and experience shows we must expect, many of the characteristic phenomena of what psychologists have called the mob mind. Moreover, administration of justice by large bodies of this sort, along with and in the intervals of political business, is necessarily cumbersome and expensive, with no corresponding advantages. Hence from the Twelve Tables (B.C. 450) to modern constitutions men have agreed in prohibiting it. The provisions of modern constitutions in this respect represent more than the influence of Aristotle and of sixteenth- and seventeenth-century theory. They represent universal experience of legislative justice wherever it has been tried.

Historical jurists, who were dominant in the science of law in the latter part of the nineteenth century, taught that the history of law was a story of the progressive realizing or unfolding of the idea of liberty in human institutions. They held that the separation of powers was a logical corollary of this idea and so judicial justice must necessarily supersede legislative and executive justice in the development of a legal system. Until the present century the de-

JUDICIAL JUSTICE

velopment of Anglo-American law appeared to conform to this theory. In the sixteenth and seventeenth centuries it was settled for the common law that the King had no part in the administration of justice. As Coke put it, causes which concern the life or inheritance or goods or fortune of the subject were not to be decided by the natural reason of the executive "but by the artificial reason and judgment of the law, as pronounced by the King's justices." In colonial America the royal governor and council were long a court, at the beginning often a court of general jurisdiction, very generally the ultimate court of review, frequently the court of chancery, and sometimes the court of probate. Also the governor was sometimes chancellor, in one province "supreme ordinary," i.e., had ultimate probate jurisdiction, and sometimes had a certain criminal jurisdiction. During the eighteenth century a system of courts was gradually established which superseded executive justice and the last remnants disappeared at the Revolution.

Thus we seemed to have achieved the ideal of a government of laws and not of men, a saying which, as has often been remarked, conceals the truth of a government of men acting by law. The nineteenth century here, as everywhere else, conceived that it could completely eliminate the personal equation in all matters affecting life, liberty, or property. We carried this to the extreme in the United States. The most striking characteristic of our public law in the last century was the completeness with which executive action was tied down by legal liability and judicial review. Despite the constitutional separation of powers, the tend-

JUSTICE ACCORDING TO LAW

ency was marked to commit to courts matters of administration which were properly executive. This attempt to refer everything to the courts and settle everything by litigation produced something very like a paralysis of administration in the United States in the last quarter of the nineteenth century. Reaction was inevitable. The reaction was accelerated by the demands of an expanding law of public utilities and the requirements of modern social legislation and the service state. The result in the present century was a rapid development of administrative boards and agencies of all kinds and incidental recurrence to official discretion rather than authoritative precepts and legal reasoning, which has brought back to our polity the long obsolete and supposedly defunct executive justice and has been making it an ordinary feature of our government.

Our polity as it had grown up in the formative era of American law, from the Revolution to the Civil War, was itself the result of a reaction. It had grown out of the administrative regime in Tudor and Stuart England and resulting conflicts between the courts and the Crown, and the administrative regime in the colonies down to the Revolution in which bodies with no separation of powers, judges of their own powers and authority, habitually acted with a high hand. In the contests of the colonists with the government at Westminster the chief reliance of Americans was on the writings of Coke and Blackstone, in which supremacy of the law and judicial scrutiny of official action to see that officials kept within the legal limits of their authority were taken to be fundamental. Like all reactions it

JUDICIAL JUSTICE

went too far and Spencer's law that action and reaction are equal and in opposite directions is illustrated in the counter-reaction in the present century. Again, there has been a tendency to go too far. The tendency has been to give to administrative agencies of every kind wide and undifferentiated powers. There has been a tendency on the part of the agencies to exercise powers of policy making and of adjudication to the verge of, if not beyond, the limits of our constitutional polity, and an increasing advocacy of administrative absolutism not only by administrative officials but by teachers and students of law and jurisprudence and politics.

At the end of the nineteenth century administrative agencies had two very real grievances against the common law and judicial review as developed under the common law in the United States. One was the common-law distinction between courts of record and tribunals not proceeding according to the course of the common law. Under English law as we received it, proceedings in a court of law, proceeding according to the course of the common law, were reviewable by writ of error upon the record of the lower tribunal. From an early date we in America assimilated other judicial tribunals to the common-law courts. They were or were made courts of record, i.e., courts in which "the proceedings were enrolled for a perpetual memorial and testimony." Where there was such a court of record its record imported verity. It could be reviewed for errors appearing on its face, but it could not be contradicted and proved itself. What it recited as having been done was established as done without more. On the other hand, where there was an administrative agency or tribunal, having no such record and not proceeding according to the course of the common law, the proceedings did not prove themselves. The proceedings and the truth of the matter recited or determined, if disputed, were to be tried in the reviewing court. Moreover, the jurisdiction of a tribunal not of record was not presumed. It had to be shown, and this meant that every fact necessary to the administrative determination might have to be shown *de novo*. Any defect in following the requirements of law might be fatal. The good sense of American courts liberalized this situation gradually to some extent. But it took legislation to do away with all its consequences and give to the proceedings of administrative agencies the weight and credence to which they were entitled.

Another grievance fifty years ago was the enforcing upon administrative tribunals of the rules of evidence developed by the common-law courts to meet the exigencies of jury trials. Provisions that the legal rules of evidence should not apply to administrative tribunals and that the proceedings should not be examined for infringement of such rules became common. These statutes, in the zeal of the draftsman to get away from technical rules of evidence, often seemed to dispense with all rules and leave such tribunals free to act without any basis in evidence of logical probative force. In some states the findings of fact made by public utility commissioners were made conclusive. In others the courts

JUDICIAL JUSTICE

in reviewing administrative proceedings were restricted to a case certified to them by the commission.

Soon the reaction went much beyond restriction of judicial power with respect to regulation of public utilities. For a generation in the present century from fifteen to twenty statutes giving wide powers of dealing with the liberty or property of individuals to administrative boards, to be exercised summarily or upon such hearings as comport with lay notions of fair play, were to be found in the annual reviews of current state legislation. Later they began to be set up by the federal government with increasing frequency.

Since 1900 the venue of litigation over private water rights, in the states where irrigation is practiced, has been shifted from the courts to state boards of engineers or administrative boards of control. Workmen's compensation legislation has taken a great mass of tort litigation largely out of the domain of adjudication and confided it to administration. It is not unlikely that injuries to passengers in railway and bus accidents and even injuries in automobile accidents may presently go the same way. Unfair competition, corporate reorganization, corporate management, and deceit in the issuing of securities have in large part gone the same way through federal legislation. Even in criminal causes, which we have thought of as par excellence the domain of the common law, juvenile courts, boards of children's guardians, probation commissions, parole commissions, and other attempts to individualize the treatment of

JUSTICE ACCORDING TO LAW

offenders, and the endeavors of the medical profession to take questions involving expert opinion out of the forum and commit them to some sort of medical referee, indicate an introduction into punitive justice of an administrative element which is alien both to our inherited ideas and to much of the lessons of Anglo-American experience. Indeed, a recent book by a professor in a law school advocates turning over murder cases to a homicide commission.

Nor has the legislature been alone in bringing back this nonjudicial element in the determination of private rights which had been all but excluded from our polity. If we look back over the course of decision since the ninth decade of the last century it will be seen that the judiciary has been falling into line and that powers which even fifty years ago would have been held purely judicial and jealously guarded from executive exercise gradually came to be held administrative and cheerfully conceded to boards and commissions. Some courts have hesitated while others have been willing to give up everything but formal actions at law and enforcement of trusts and prevention of torts in equity where there is threat of irreparable injury, and even the latter in case of labor disputes.

Before 1880 the state courts generally held to an overrigid analytical doctrine as to the separation of powers and in consequence tended to hold all matters involving a hearing and determination, whereby the liberty, property, or fortune of an individual might be affected, to be exclusively judicial. After 1880, the cases, at first requiring a possibility of appeal or of judicial review but later casting off more and more of that remnant of the older doctrine, have tended more and more to hold every sort of power which does not involve directly an adjudication of a controversy between man and man, and in some cases, such as disputes over water rights, those which do, to be administrative in character and legitimate matter for commissions or bureaus.

Let me give some examples. Disputes over water rights, where the conflicting claims of numerous appropriators threatened to give rise to a multiplicity of suits, were first taken in hand by courts of equity. Later statutes were enacted whereby the power to determine the nature, priority, and effect of the several appropriations and to apportion the use of the stream was given to a state engineer or to some administrative board. In 1870 the pioneer statute of this kind was held unconstitutional on the ground that the power conferred was judicial. But before a quarter of a century had passed the courts were agreed, quite rightly, that the power was not exclusively judicial and such statutes were upheld. Again, the older decisions were reluctant to concede to executive boards any power of hearing and determining charges against public officers and of removing them after such hearing. Later cases settled, quite properly, that this power of removal after investigation may be given to executive officers or boards of legislation. As late as 1883 a statute giving a board of county commissioners power to hear and determine complaints against holders of licenses and to revoke licenses thereupon was held bad as giving judicial power to executive functionaries. Subject to requirements of due process of law such statutes are now

JUSTICE ACCORDING TO LAW

rightly upheld. Today very wide powers as to parole, probation, and transfer of convicts by administrative agencies are upheld.

I have no doubt that this change in the course of decision is perfectly sound. I am not preaching against administrative agencies in themselves. The society of today demands services beyond those that the state which only maintained order and repaired injuries could perform. In a complex industrial society it becomes more and more difficult to do by private initiative many things which the public wishes done and done quickly. Administrative agencies of promoting the general welfare have come to be a necessity and have come to stay. It would be futile to quarrel with the idea of a service state kept in balance with the idea of individual spontaneous initiative characteristic of the American. But conceding this we do not concede the further changes often urged on behalf of administrative boards and agencies which would relieve them from effective judicial scrutiny of their action to see that they keep within their statutory powers, that they interpret and apply rightly the law governing their action in a particular case, that they in reality and not in pretence apply the standard committed to them, and that their actions and proceedings conform to due process of law. Nor can we concede that review when allowed for the purposes just set forth shall be committed solely to administrative superiors or administrative courts. There is an observable tendency of administrative agencies to substitute shaping of policy to the exigencies of vaguely conceived ideas of public good for the

JUDICIAL JUSTICE

legislative pronouncement by which their action is supposed to be governed. It is not only a matter of keeping judicial power in the judiciary but also of keeping lawmaking power in the legislature. There are those in our law schools today who advocate a complete fusion of legislative, executive, and judicial power in administrative boards and bureaus and agencies. Even without constitutional amendment authorizing this, administrative agencies are not unlikely to attain it in substance unless judicial scrutiny of their action can be preserved and made effective.

What differentiates administrative adjudication from judicial justice is the lack of checks upon arbitrary, biased, or extra-legal if not unlawful (in the sense of lack of accord with the legal rights of individuals) action in the one case as compared with the numerous and effective checks in the other.

In the best discussion of administrative adjudication I have been able to find in the books we are told there are six checks upon the process. One is said to be that the administrative as distinguished from the judicial process moves in a narrow field and so "is not open to the broad range of human sympathies to which the judicial process is open." But this is not a check. The confining of determinations to a highly specialized field leads to looking at all things from the standpoint of that narrow field and so to ignoring one side of disputed questions of fact in view of supposed exigencies of that field, a fault which is unhappily very common in administrative determinations. Second, it is said that this concern only with a narrow field develops a professional attitude which is a better guarantee of informed and balanced judgments than legal precepts or legal reasoning. On the contrary, this preoccupation with a narrow field is one of the chief reasons why effective judicial review of administrative determinations to hold them within the limits of due process of law is urgently demanded by lawyers. Exclusive concern with a narrow field easily closes the mind of the official to much that bears on the facts to be ascertained. Third, we are told that there is a check in the requirement, often made by statute, that there be findings of fact made. But too often there are no effective means of assuring a proper basis for the findings in evidence of rational probative force after full hearing of all sides and opportunity to refute or explain everything used in arriving at the adverse finding. A fourth check is said to be in the relation of adjudication to policy. Experience shows that so far from being a check, here is in part a source of one of the most flagrant abuses in administrative determination, namely, determination of facts not on the basis of hearing and evidence but on the basis of preconceptions of facts to fit the assumed exigencies of a policy. Many examples of this which are not controversial may be seen in the findings of prohibition administrators under the National Prohibition Act. But we could match them with findings of administrative agencies today in every volume of the *Federal Reporter*. A fifth check is said to be promised in that in the development of administrative law the administrative process is divorced from the executive by setting up independent tribunals. But if such

JUDICIAL JUSTICE

tribunals are set up they will not have the constitutional guarantee of independence that the courts have. They will be dependent upon the legislature and the executive, not coequal with legislature and executive as are the courts of justice set up by the Constitution. Finally, sixth, the author cites the check of judicial review. But he hastens to add that the tendency has been to narrow and often to preclude judicial review. In truth, it is not allowed to be the check that it ought to be.

There is a marked tendency in administrative agencies to see the relatively narrow task of the particular agency out of proportion. For an example no longer controversial, those who administered the National Prohibition Act felt, no doubt conscientiously, that the objects of that act were of such paramount importance as to justify extra-legal measures and overriding of individual rights and constitutional guarantees. Excess of zeal in carrying out laws, which are felt by administrative agencies to be of such vital importance as to justify the means by the end is one of the reasons why the American constitutional polity is by no means obsolete. The fundamental features of government it was set up to deal with are as much in need of restraint today as they ever were. In a constitutional legal polity all exercise of the power of politically organized society calls for checks.

That checks are peculiarly needed with respect to administrative adjudication is made clear by certain general and persistent tendencies of administrative agencies, federal and state, as well as in like agencies in England and

JUSTICE ACCORDING TO LAW

in the British Dominions. Perhaps the most serious is a tendency to decide without a hearing, or without hearing one of the parties, or by a mere appearance of a hearing—going through the appearance of one, the results having been predetermined. One form of this is to give full credence to all the testimony on one and deny it to everything testified to on the other side. Courts have called attention to this repeatedly in the last few years. A closely related tendency is to make determinations on the basis of consultations with witnesses in private or of reports not divulged, giving the party affected no opportunity to refute or explain. No less serious is a tendency to make determinations injuriously affecting individual rights without a basis in evidence of rational probative force. Also there is a tendency no less widespread, but much more difficult to reach by judicial review under the statutes and procedure of today, to set up and give effect to policies beyond or even at variance with the statutes or the general law governing the action of the administrative agency. It is easy to say that the public interest calls for activity beyond or in contravention of the statute and to cover this up by a general pronouncement upon the case. It results from zeal to promote social ends to which the legislature might not agree. It involves a degree of legislative power in administrative agencies which is not given them and ought not to be given them.

Much has been done for a check upon federal administrative agencies by the Federal Administrative Procedure Act. But there is much that it does not reach, as one may see brought out in every volume of the *Federal Reporter*. Advocates of administrative absolutism decry all pointing out of highhanded and one-sided administrative action as "reactionary." Enthusiastic believers in the service state as an omnicompetent agency of perfecting society assume that its bureaus do only what they are set up to do and do it as they are set up to do it. Even a scintilla of the "realism" they apply to the courts, if turned to the cases where the courts are called on to review administrative adjudications, might surprise them.

Administrative law is something new in the common-law world. Our administrative tribunals have no such taught tradition of experience developed by reason behind them as have our courts or the administrative agencies of Continental Europe. To develop and systematize such a taught tradition and fit it to our political and legal tradition of the supremacy of the law is the task of American jurists.

We are careful about checks where administrative powers are given to lower courts and especially where they are given to new types of court with a large grant of discretion. A series of checks are imposed upon such judicial administration and the fullest review before a bench of judges is afforded.

Our Anglo-American legal system is characteristically judicial, as the Continental system is characteristically administrative. The bigness of things today and the rise of the service state call for a large growth of administration. But a dominant administration, not checked by law applied by an independent judiciary, means a mere preach-

JUSTICE ACCORDING TO LAW

ment bill of rights, a hierarchy of superman administrative officials who ex officio know what is good for us better than we know ourselves, and ultimately a super-superman to give direction to and maintain order and eliminate friction in the hierarchy. It is significant that some European countries which have had experience of a judiciary part of the executive and have seen in their neighbors or at home what absolute administrative government means are now setting up independent judicial tribunals to give effect to the Declaration of Rights.

In legal history setting off of the judicial function has been a gradual process. The Roman polity to the end confided judicial power to the ordinary magistrates. Under the later empire the judges were subordinate magistrates from whom an appeal lay to the emperor. On the Continent, in the Middle Ages justice was administered by what were also legislative assemblies which later became courts, and with the reception of Roman law the idea of the judge was taken from Rome. In England, an independent judiciary grew up in the Middle Ages. The judges exercised the royal power of keeping the King's peace and vindicating the King's authority and it became settled that the King could not administer justice in person nor sit in the courts. At the Revolution of 1688 independence of the judges was thoroughly established. The English judge had the prestige of royal authority. He stood for the King. The Roman *judex* had only appointment by the *praetor* (judicial magistrate) behind him. In the later empire the person who decided was a subordinate magistrate, not the immediate perma-

JUDICIAL JUSTICE

nent representative of the sovereign. In America, we inherited the idea of independent courts and the supremacy of the law and put them in all of our constitutions.

Objections to judicial justice today have been chiefly directed to the law-finding or law-declaring function of common-law judges. But this function cannot be separated from the functions of interpreting the law and applying the law. Hence objections which have been made as to every phase of judicial administration of justice may be taken up together.

It has always been urged against judicial justice that it is too rigid, too hard and fast; that it trusts too much to rule and does not allow sufficient play to the nonlegal conscience in ascertaining or in applying the law. This is but another form of one of the stock complaints against justice according to law. It comes really to the proposition that judicial justice realizes justice according to law most completely and so brings out its difficulties as well as its good features. There was a tendency in the United States at one time to temper judicial exercise of the deciding function by conceding extravagant powers to juries. There was a real ground of complaint in the last century in the days of what has been called mechanical jurisprudence, when attempt was made to reduce everything to detailed rule. This was characteristic of legislation and administration as well as judicial decision. It was not inherent in the judicial process and has disappeared.

Objection is made also to the premises employed in judicial justice. It is urged that they are too narrow and

JUSTICE ACCORDING TO LAW

pedantic; that the starting points for reasoning are too fixed so that judicial justice is too slow in responding to changes in the environment in which it must operate. This assumes a judicial function of general instead of what Mr. Justice Holmes called interstitial lawmaking. Unfortunately both English and American judges today are embarrassed by public expectation of more than they are well fitted to do because of failure of legislatures to do the work of lawmaking which belongs to them in our polity. Ilbert tells us that Parliament is not interested in lawyer's law. Mr. Justice Cardozo has commented on the neglect of legislatures to provide the authoritative materials for decision which would enable courts to do their work with assurance. There is no political advantage for individual members in promoting legislation for improvement of everyday law. Economic questions and legislative investigations and partisan political wrangling over allocation of funds for public works among local communities take up the time and energy of legislators if for no other reason because the publicity which is the best asset of the politician is involved here rather than in details of reform of the law. There is need of a ministry of justice in the state to do the work of preparation which would enable the legislature to perform adequately what the separation of powers expects of it. The heavy pressure upon courts today to do what ought to be the work of legislatures is a hindrance to judicial justice. Attempt to control application of law by minute and detailed legislation is a mistake. On the other hand, attempt to set up new premises for legal reasoning on a

JUDICIAL JUSTICE

large scale by judicial lawmaking impairs the stability of the legal and so of the economic order. Judicial development of law proceeds by analogical reasoning, that is, in effect by choice between competing analogies in the authoritative body of legal precepts. New premises suggesting new analogies may more or less unsettle the legal system. New starts, therefore, are better made by legislation which has no retroactive application and may be fitted into the system judicially by experience without unsettling the transactions of the past.

A third objection which has been made to judicial justice is that it has been characterized by a tendency to reduce to rule, along with those things which demand rule, those with respect to which detailed rules are not practicable. Thus in the last century courts sought to reduce the details of procedure, evidence, administrative law, and the law as to negligence to chapter and verse of strict rule. But this was a tendency of the nineteenth century in every connection. The legislation of the New York Code of Civil Procedure went far beyond any judicial course of decision in the attempt to subject every detail of what went on in court to fixed rule. Legislation long tried to tie down administration quite as tight as judicial decision ever sought to do. The attempt of the courts in the last century to reduce everything to rule only represents one phase of the mechanical thinking which characterized all the social sciences during that period.

Turning to the advantages of judicial justice, in the first place, with respect both to the law-declaring and to the

JUSTICE ACCORDING TO LAW

deciding function, it combines the possibilities of certainty and of flexibility better than any other form of administering justice. It provides for certainty through training of the judge in logical development and systematic exposition of authoritative materials for decision. It provides for growth by permitting a scientific testing of received starting points for legal reasoning with reference to concrete cases and correction of precepts by extension or restriction through experience of their application and a gradual process of inclusion and exclusion upon rational principles.

Secondly, there are checks upon judges which do not obtain or are ineffective as to legislators and executive officials. Four such checks are of especial importance. One is that the judge from his very training is impelled to conform his action to certain known principles or standards. Professional habit leads him in every case to seek such principles or standards before acting and to refer his action thereto. Second, every decision is subject to criticism by a trained profession, to whose opinion the judge, as a member of the profession, is keenly sensitive. Third, every decision and the case on which it was based, the claims of the parties, the evidence, and the findings of fact, appear in public records. Moreover, in case of appellate courts all important decisions and the grounds thereof and reason therefor are published in the law reports so that materials for accurate judgment upon judicial decisions are always available and always accessible. Fourth, decisions of judges of first instance are reviewable by a bench of judges and in appellate courts a judge sits as one of a bench and must

JUDICIAL JUSTICE

take part with his colleagues in decision so that individual prejudices and preconceptions and eccentricities get ironed out.

A third advantage of judicial justice is that judges will on the whole uphold the law against excitement and clamor. They do so because of their training in the law, because of their habit of seeking and applying principles whenever called upon to act, and because of consciousness that their decisions will be preserved in permanent form and will be subject to expert criticism in the future as well as to popular criticism in the present. Training and consciousness that the legal soundness or unsoundness of decisions will be apparent to the bar at once in ordinary cases and to jurists and law teachers in unusual cases, operate both as a check and as a stimulus. Consequently judicial justice has always proved the surest agency of enforcing the law in case of opposition. The "legislative lynchings" of loyalists during and after the Revolution should be compared with the steadfastness with which judges protected them in their legal rights even when threatened with popular vengeance. The legislative and executive treatment of outlanders in the South African Republic which led to the Boer War should be compared with the firm stand for law taken by the Chief Justice of the Transvaal in the face of an arbitrary executive. Chief Justice Kotze was removed by President Kruger for enforcing the Grondwet (fundamental law) as chief justices were removed by the Stuart kings for enforcing adherence to Magna Carta. In each case the arbitrary executives were overthrown. Under national prohibi-

JUSTICE ACCORDING TO LAW

tion the so-called padlock injunctions were by far the most effective means of enforcement. Such cases as the enforcement of the Fugitive Slave Law by state courts in the North just before the Civil War are significant. The judges were abused for enforcing that law, as required of them by the federal constitution, by those who equally denounced secession. Not a little denunciation of judges has proceeded from those who did not wish the law to operate equally and exactly, but wished to see it warped in their favor and resented judicial resistance to pressure under which administrative officials would yield.

The picture of the Anglo-American judge which I have sketched is not, I am well aware, the one drawn in recent years by the self-styled realists. But I suggest to you that so-called realism in jurisprudence is related to realism in art rather than to philosophical realism. Like realism in art it is a cult of the ugly. The realist in art says the ugly exists in nature, therefore it is true. So to be true I must paint the ugly. But when he says the ugly is real he may mean it exists, which no one can deny, or he may mean that it is significant, which is disputable. An artist commissioned to paint the portrait of one of the outstanding judges of the recent past noted that he had a huge fist and a habit of holding it out before him. Accordingly, as a realist, he painted the fist elaborately in the foreground as the chief feature of the portrait, behind which, if one's gaze can get by the fist, one may discover in the background a thoughtful countenance. The judge did have such a fist and did hold it out in front of him on occasion. But having known him well for years, I doubt if any one thought about it till the artist seized upon it and made it the main feature of his portrait. The fist existed. But was it the significant feature of the judge? Was reality in the sense of significance in the fist or in the countenance?

So it is with juristic realism. We have always known that the judicial process does not at all times and in all places conform absolutely and in all respects to our ideal of it. Despite all the checks with which we surround it, it does not come out in every case entirely as we could wish. But the striving for the ideal, I repeat, goes far to realize the ideal. It is the approximation to our ideal of it which is significant, not the fallings short, which we seek continually to control and to reduce to a minimum. If a theory of social control through the force of politically organized society is made from the fallings short rather than from the achievements, we shall undo what has made increasingly for civilization since the beginnings of modern law in the later Middle Ages.

We must bear in mind that theories of the impossibility of justice according to law and of the disappearance of law have largely gone along with, have developed side by side with, absolute theories in politics. The two are concomitants of the movement toward absolute government which has been going on in every part of the world. The theories of law in terms of threat and force are part of a general cult of force. The real foe of absolutism is law. It presupposes a life measured by reason, a legal order measured by reason, and a judicial process carried on by applying a reasoned technique to experience developed by reason and reason tested by experience.

INDEX

Absolute government, movement toward, 91
Acton, Lord, 18
Administration, tying down of in nineteenth century, 71–72
Administrative absolutism, 83
Administrative agencies: checks upon, 76–81; grievances of, 73–75; necessity of, 78; tendencies of, 78–79, 81–82
Administrative tribunals: checks upon, 76–81; common-law restrictions of, 73–75; growth of, 25; increasing jurisdiction of, 76–78; need of checks on, 81–83; want of taught tradition, 83
Aerial navigation, 53
American law, formative era of, 71–73
Ames, James Barr, 10
Analogy, 60; reasoning from, 51–53
Anglo-Saxon law, 58

Appeals to legislature, 66–67
Aquinas, St. Thomas, 18
Aristotle, 4, 5, 9, 18–19, 63
Attainder, acts of, 66

Bacon, 1
Bailment, 58
Bentham, 25
Bill of rights, 84
Blackstone, 7, 63, 72

Cardozo, 35, 45, 49, 86
Causation, 10, 14
Civil law, tradition of, 60–61
Coke, 71, 72
College fraternities, 17–18
Common carrier, 57
Common law, tradition of, 60–61
Common owners, 15
Compromise, 29–30
Comte, 28
Conceptions, legal, 58
Conduct, channeling of, 17
Connecticut, 66, 68
Cooley, Judge, 7
Courts, checks upon, 88–89
Courts not of record, 73–74
Criminal investigation, 23
Criminal law, 22
Culture state, 22

Declaration of Independence, 63
Democracy, realist theory of, 35
Dicey, 29
Discretion, 43
Divorce, legislative, 66; Alabama, 66; Pennsylvania, 66, 68; Rhode Island, 66, 68
Due process of law, 55–56, 59
Duguit, 28

Economic realism, 35
Einstein, 36
End of law, theories of, 28–30
Epicurus, 23
Equitable mortgage, 52
Ethelbert, laws of, 58
Evidence, rules of, 74–75
Executive justice, 65; in American colonies, 71; revival of, 73–78

Fault, 10–12
Freedom of contract, 26
French Civil Code, 7, 51
Fugitive Slave Law, 90

German Civil Code, 7
Gibson, John Bannister, 37–38
Good Samaritan, 23
Government of laws, 71
Greek philosophers, 43
Grotius, 24, 27

Hammurabi, 56
Harun-al-Raschid, 32–33
Henry II, 33
Historical school, 25–26, 47, 70
Hobbes, 24
Holmes, 45, 86
House of Lords, as court, 65–66

Ideal element of law, 54–56
Ilbert, 86

INDEX

Independent contractor, 13–14
Independent judiciary: growth of in England, 84–85; need of, 84
Institutes of Justinian, 3
Interpretation, 55
Ius, 40

James, William, 30–31
Johnson, Dr. Samuel, 18
Judges: effect of taught tradition on, 37–39; English and Continental compared, 84–85
Judicial function, 65; setting off of, 84
Judicial justice: advantages of, 87–90; as agency of enforcement, 89–90; checks upon, 88–89; objections to, 85–87
Judicial process, 49; fallings short of, 91
Judicial review, 77, 78
Judicial tribunals, checks upon inferior, 83
Jurisdiction, giving up to administrative agencies, 76–79
Jurisprudence of phrases, 59
Jury, extravagant powers of, 86
Justice: administration of, 16–18; Aristotle's theory of, 9; as a moral idea, 6–16; as end of law, 28–29; as realizing law, 18; Bentham's idea of, 25; commutative, 9, 18–19; definitions of, 2, 3, 29; distributive, 9, 19; Greek theories of, 2–5, 19; historical theory of, 25–26; Kantian idea of, 24; medieval theory of, 19; nineteenth-century idea of, 6; Radbruch's definition, 19; theory of Greek philosophers, 19; theory of Spanish jurist-theologians, 19–21; utilitarian idea of, 25; value theory of, 21–23
Justinian, 7

Kant, 5, 26; idea of justice, 24
King, as judge, 71
Kotze, Chief Justice, 89

Law, as a form of social control, 19; as aggregate of laws, 59–60; as taught tradition, 60; canon of value theory of, 46; command theory of, 44; definition of, 43–48; elements of, 50–59; end of, 28–31; Greek idea of, 43; historical idea of, 47; ideal element of, 54–56; ideas of, 39–43; lawyer's idea of, 48–49; meaning of, 39–56; model of decision theory of, 44; need of, 32–35; power theory of, 46; precept element of, 51–59; prediction theory of, 44–45; realist idea of, 49, 62; realist theory of, 35–36; rule-of-conduct theory of, 44; St. Paul on, 61; sociologist idea of, 47; standpoints from which defined, 43–46; technique element of, 50–54; the

Law (*continued*)
real foe of absolutism, 91; threat theory of, 44; three meanings of, 48; traditional element of, 41–43; unification of meanings of, 49–50
Lawmaking, judicial, 86–87
Law-of-nature school, 23–24
Law state, 22
Legal order, 16–27, 50, 98; theory of in antiquity, 20–21
Legislation: analogy of, 50–52; province of, 40–43
Legislative justice, 65–70; bad features of, 67–69; obsolescence of, 67; supposed advantages of, 69–70
Legislature, failure to make needed laws, 86
Leibniz, 24, 27
Letter-of-credit cases, 52–53
Lex, 40
Lex aeterna, 19
Liability: absolute, 13; for causation, 10, 14; for fault, 10–12; for servants and agents, 11; insurance theory of, 11–13; vicarious, 11; without fault, 10–14, 54–55
Libel, Dicey on, 29–30
Liberty, 20–26, 27
Licenses, revocation of, 77–78
Llewellyn, 46
Locke, 24
Loss, burden of, 9, 11–13
Louis IX, 33
Lyndhurst, Lord, 65

Maine, 25–26, 45
Maritain, 14–15
Marshall, Chief Justice, 64
Maryland, 66
Melville, Lord, impeachment of, 66
Metaphysical school, 24–25
Middle Ages, theory of justice in, 19
Ministry of justice, 86
Montesquieu, 63

National Prohibition Act, 80
Natural law, 6, 14–16, 19
Neo-Hegelians, 28
Neo-Kantians, 23
Neo-realists, 35
Neo-Scholasticism, 28
Neo-Thomists, 28
New trials, legislative, 66–67
New York, 66–67

O'Connell outlawry case, 65
Overruling of decisions, 59–60
Ownership to the zenith, 53

Padlock injunctions, 50
Pains and penalties, bills of, 66
Philosophers: Epicureans, 1; Neo-Idealists, 1; New Academy, 1; Pragmatists, 1; Thomists, 1
Philosophical jurists, 64
Pilate, 1
Plato, 3, 43
Positivism, 28
Principle, defined, 56–57

INDEX

Privy Council, authority of in colonies, 63
Property, 41–42
Psychological realism, 36
Public policy, 10–11
Public service, 57
Public utilities, law of, 72
Pufendorf, 24
Pyrrho, 23

Queen Caroline case, 66

Radbruch, 19, 21–22, 23, 24
Radicalism, juristic, 26–27
Realism, juristic and absolute government, 91
Realism, juristic, 35–39, 62–63, 90–91
Religious procession case, 33–35
Right, meanings of, 2, 39–40
Right, vested to job, 39
Rights, realist theory of, 35
Roman law, 7, 46–47, 51
Rousseau, 24
Royal governor, as judge, 71
Ruffin, Thomas, 38
Rule and discretion, 40–43, 65
Rule, defined, 56
Rules, short life of, 60

St. Augustine, 23
St. Paul, 61
Sale, 58
Salic law, 56
Security, new meaning of, 29

Separation of powers, 63–65; analytical view of, 64; historical theory of, 70
Service state, 29, 73, 78, 83
Shaw, Lemuel, 37
Sidgwick, 5
Social control, 49–50; agencies of, 16–18; task of, 31
Social engineering, 30
Social-philosophical schools, 28
Sociological jurists, idea of law, 47
Sociologists, idea of law, 47
Socrates, 43
South African Republic, executive justice in, 89
Spanish jurist-theologians, 19–21, 23
Specific relief, 53
Spencer, 26, 73
Standards, application of, 55–56
State: culture, 27; law, 27; prerogative of dishonesty, 69
Status quo, social, 17–18
Status to contract, 25–26
Stop, look, and listen rule, 59
Substance, interests of, 41
Succession, 41

Taught tradition: of Continental universities, 60–61; of Inns of Court, 61; of Roman jurisconsults, 61; vitality of, 60–61
Technique: civil law, 51–54; common law, 51–54, 60
Text writers, 59–60
Torts, 41, 54

Trust, 58
Truth, 1–2
Twelve Tables, 56, 70

Utilitarians, 25, 26

Value, canons of, 46–47
Values, theories of, 21–23

Water rights, 75, 77
Webster, Daniel, 2
Wolff, 24